praise

KABUL GIRLS

"The young Afghan women in K.... ....
neers. Their story is one of resilience and courage. This book is a
testament to the power of hope and the will to dream in a country
where so many dreams have been cut short."

—Khaled Hosseini, bestselling author of *The Kite Runner*

"As our world continues to flatten, sports, particularly soccer, has
the power to break down cultural barriers that may have existed
for generations. The courageous stories in *Kabul Girls Soccer Club*
teach us all that soccer has no boundaries, and that it can change
lives. These young girls prove to us all that while we have our own
individual identities off the field, on the field we are universally the
same—striving and struggling to achieve our greatest potential."

—Sunil Gulati, President of the U.S. Soccer Federation

"*Kabul Girls Soccer Club* is a testament to the power of sports and
the impact it can have on young girls throughout the world."

—Julie Foudy,
former Captain of the U.S. Women's National Soccer Team

"How do you tell the varied stories of eight fiery Afghan teenagers
as well as the life journey of their American-raised sponsor? The
red thread that weaves through all these lives is not the game of
soccer itself but a stubborn will to contend in the face of limited
resources, family disapproval, and public harassment . . . The courage of these eight girls will inspire readers of all backgrounds."

—*Library Journal*

kabul girls

SOCCER CLUB

kabul girls
SOCCER CLUB

A DREAM, EIGHT GIRLS,

AND A JOURNEY HOME

Awista Ayub

HYPERION

NEW YORK

To my parents

Mohammad Hassan Ayub and Bibi Aissa Ayub (Gulalai),

the girls' soccer team of Afghanistan,

& the eight girls who began it all

Contents

Author's Note

LIKE THE AFGHANISTAN girls' soccer team, this book was the product of a collaborative effort. I want to thank two people without whom this book would not have been made, Veronica Golos and Sophia Hollander.

As a poet and editor, Veronica Golos brought to the book a keen editing eye, and a deep understanding of and extensive research about Afghanistan. Her attention to language and nuance—and her extraordinary patience—helped to add a literary dimension to the book.

And writer Sophia Hollander was instrumental in the writing of the first draft of this book. She traveled with me to Kabul and came to understand not only these girls, but the culture of Afghanistan. Through the intense hours of interviews and research, the stories of the girls would not have been as true without her contribution.

It is to them that I am most grateful.

Note to the Reader

TODAY, AFGHANISTAN IS in the throes of grappling with the profound issue of the type of country it will become. This healthy self-questioning in the aftermath of nearly three decades of war brings with it conflict and debates about the preservation of tradition versus modernity, and has descended at times into harsh accusations and actions.

To protect the girls, aspects of their stories have been changed—including names and certain identifying details.

The first-person narratives are based on my memories, bolstered by interviews with those who experienced it with me including (but not limited to) the girls, coaches, school administrators, Afghan officials, and my own family. The chapters of the girls reflect extensive interviews with each girl and her family. These stories are as accurate as memory—and my knowledge of their lives and households—can make them.

Still, at times, nailing down the exact dates or chronology was a challenge, as sustained war has destroyed records, along with the country's school system.

Throughout this book, I have sought to capture each of their lives as truthfully as possible, while preserving their privacy, security, and personal peace.

"However tall the mountain, there's always a road."
—AFGHAN PROVERB

AFTER BEING BUILT in 1923, Afghanistan's Ghazi Stadium in Kabul became the site of numerous men's national team soccer games and national celebrations. But from 1996 to 2001, during the Taliban regime, those caught stealing, committing acts of adultery, or even lesser offenses were punished openly on the stadium grounds. Men and women were brutally executed in front of crowds gathered at the stadium, as a reminder of the fate that would befall anyone who dared to make the same mistakes.

Today, while the memories of the executions are not yet forgotten, Ghazi Stadium has once again returned to its glory hosting national parades, but this time the crowds also gather in support of Afghanistan's first women's national soccer team. Though the struggle for freedom continues, there is a glimmer of hope on the green fields within Ghazi's walls.

kabul girls

SOCCER CLUB

Dream

The white ball bounces down a stark rutted slope in Kabul's Old City, dust rising in a plume as it tumbles past a well surrounded by a gaggle of children, their water pails glinting in the intense sun. The ball careens off a series of footholds carved by hands or geology—or a recent explosion. From behind plastic-sheeted windows, in brick clay homes perched precariously on the hillside, curious eyes follow the falling globe.

Almost red with dust, the soccer ball finally stops on the well-traveled dirt path below. Three boys, thin and laughing, stop also, and stare—as if it had been dropped from heaven.

"A soccer ball," one boy exclaims.

"Whose is it?" asks another.

The boys look around, squint up the hillside.

"Let's play!" yells the third.

Thirty feet above, a girl watches the boys with amusement. She sips from her cup of tea. "I'll get the ball later," she says to herself. "And show them how to kick it."

prologue

 N THE MORNING of April 28, 1978, my father woke up to the radio's newscast: "The previous government has been removed and the new revolutionary government now represents the people of Afghanistan." The Marxist Afghan-led People's Democratic Party of Afghanistan (PDPA) had launched a coup against the government of Mohammed Daoud Khan, who—along with most of his family—had been shot inside the Presidential Palace.

Overnight, life changed for millions of Afghans. The coup divided the country, fractured families and friendships.

Within a week, my father lost his engineering job.

Soon after, a former colleague of his from the Ministry of Power and Water stopped him at the bazaar. "Your life is in danger," he told my father. "You should have supported the regime in a more 'demonstrative' manner."

My father didn't wait to see what would happen; he went straight to see his father-in-law, Mohammad Iss-haq Babai, who refused to acknowledge the new government, or the redistribution they planned for his five hundred acres.

"Things are getting bad," my father pleaded. "We must save our lives. Please, the entire family should flee to Pakistan."

"What? You want me to leave my house, my city, my country, to go and live there?" Babai replied. "I will never do it."

"But I am going and I am taking my family with me."

My grandfather, unwilling to leave his land, was shot and killed outside of his home in Kandahar a few months after my father left the country.

My father left for Pakistan from Kandahar. Riding on the back of a motorcycle, whose driver he'd paid to help him cross the border, he bypassed the main roads and headed for Quetta, Pakistan—a 115-mile ride through rough back roads, so as to avoid military checkpoints. Helicopters prowled the border constantly.

Once inside Pakistan, my father went to the U.S. Embassy in Islamabad and joined the thousands of Afghans massed outside hoping to come to the United States. He was right to have traveled alone. It would have been nearly impossible in the chaos of so many clamoring for passage to have his wife and three young children with him. He waited outside from early morning to evening for two weeks, amid much pushing and shoving, part of the hazard of getting noticed. Finally, he was able to get a meeting.

Thinking it might help, he'd brought his papers from an

irrigation training program he'd attended at the University of Hawaii. This connection proved to be enough; embassy officials agreed to allow our family to emigrate.

With no phone system, fax machines, or working postal service in Afghanistan, it was typical at the time to ask someone to hand deliver messages and letters. My father found a young boy traveling to Kabul.

"If I give you this letter," he asked, "can you give it to my brother?"

The boy agreed.

⚜

MY MOTHER AND her three young children were temporarily living with her mother-in-law and brother-in-law in the Karte Se district of Kabul. On receiving the letter, she bundled us up, gathered a bag of clothing, and then headed on a plane back to Kandahar, where her mother and sister were living. She spent a frantic week searching for a way to cross the border.

She finally found another family in a nearby village preparing to leave also. We were all to escape on a farmer's trailer. To pay the 1,000 afghani ($200) fee the farmer charged per person, my mother pulled together all she had saved as a teacher and sold her jewelry.

We set off at sunset. My mother, my siblings and me, and my aunt lay crouched and crowded on the metal bed of the trailer. My grandmother decided to stay in Afghanistan, along with two other families.

We didn't dare turn on the lights, so the trailer slowly

blundered into the darkness. It was cold. The roads ahead were heavily mined; two men on motorcycles crept ahead searching for trip wires that could kill us all.

The helicopters rumbled overhead, their search beams sweeping across the darkened roads. Explosions burst across the landscape in brilliant, terrifyingly bright blasts.

Concealed beneath a canvas covering, my mother anticipated the impact of a bomb from above, or instant death from a tripped mine exploding below. Placing her body over us, eyes closed, she imagined that at any moment the canvas might be torn away, exposing us to soldiers.

We rode all night. That next morning, we crossed the border into Quetta, Pakistan. My father met us there. After weeks of waiting, our family flew to America, our new "temporary" home.

꩜

BUT THE WARS continued. Temporary became permanent. For my parents *permanent* was fused with a desire to return to the country they remembered. Throughout my childhood, I traveled to Afghanistan—in my imagination.

Then, overnight, my world changed: In 2001, the United States entered Afghanistan and overthrew the Taliban.

Suddenly, it seemed possible for me to go back there. But visiting would not be enough. I didn't want to be a tourist in my own homeland. I wanted to make a meaningful contribution to the country in which I'd been born.

꩜

OUT OF THAT longing was also born an idea and, subsequently, this book.

In the pages that follow, you will meet eight courageous Afghan girls and learn of their journey to America and back home. This book is about my own journey too. About being Afghan-American, and how that hyphen includes and divides. You will come to understand the great belief of all cultures: that beneath our myriad differences, we are one.

This book is about hope. Hope in its most muscular sense. Because, however tall the mountain, there's always a road.

1

reborn

AMERICA, JUNE 2004

THAT SUMMER EVENING, the sky was ablaze with stars, the air humid and cloudless. Pacing the lawn outside my friend Barbara Goodno's suburban Washington, D.C., home, I asked myself: *Are they ready?*

Eight months earlier I had come up with the idea to sponsor a group of eight girls from Afghanistan to the United States for a soccer leadership camp. Now, they were here for six weeks, spending two weeks in Washington, D.C., the remaining weeks in Connecticut where I'd organized a soccer camp, and then finally traveling to Cleveland, Ohio, to represent Afghanistan in the International Children's Games.

After only two weeks in America, with just a handful of formal practices, the girls from Afghanistan would be playing their first-ever public soccer game.

Laila. Freshta. Samira. Miriam.
Deena. Nadia. Ariana. Robina.

Earlier, the girls prepared their uniforms. Each had folded her red jersey with the white numbers facing up. Underneath the shirts, they tucked red socks, black shorts, and cleats. The neat piles were lined outside their rooms in a row down the hall.

The next day, these eight girls would be competing in the Seventh Annual Fourth of July Afghan-American Soccer Cup tournament, sponsored and organized by the Afghan Sports Federation. Founded in 1997, the three-day event drew Afghan-Americans from as far away as California and Canada not only to compete in soccer and volleyball, the two most popular sports in Afghanistan, but also to enjoy Afghan music and food.

But this was the first time there would be an *all-girls* soccer competition.

࿇

I DROVE THE girls to South Run Park in Springfield, Virginia. It had rained earlier in the morning. The fields were still damp, the sky overcast. The girls were quiet. They spread out, surveying the vast green playing fields before them.

The perimeter of the park was lined with the colorful tents of vendors. Afghan kebobs of marinated lamb, chicken, and beef—well seasoned with paprika and garlic, and skewered with tomatoes, onions, and peppers—slowly turned on their spits. I was looking forward to a bowl of *shor-nakhud,*

chopped boiled potatoes, and beans mixed with vinegar, garlic, and spices.

A crowd mingled on the grounds, lining up five or six
deep around the edges of a field where a game was due to
begin. Others picnicked in family groups, sitting on lawn
chairs and multihued quilts spread on the ground. Older Afghan women, with their flowing trousers and *hijab*, or head
scarves, took charge of laying out the food.

Pashto and Dari, the two principal languages of Afghanistan, could be heard everywhere, along with the traditional
Arabic greeting of peace:

"Assalam alaykom!" Peace be with you.

"Alaykom assalam." And with you.

"Stari me shey!"—a Pashto hello.

"Che hal dared?" How are you? (Some of the girls turned
toward the familiar Dari phrase.)

"Khub astom tashakor." Fine, thank you.

The Afghan girls drew curious glances as we meandered
around the park. They were wearing their jerseys, sleeves
below the elbow, long shorts hanging below the knees, and
socks pulled up under the shorts.

I didn't think the stares were because the players were
from Afghanistan; more likely they were because this was
an all-girls soccer team.

Miriam and Deena walked with their arms around each
other's waist. As we strolled, the other girls turned around
and around, as if unsure how to react.

Aware of the attention, while pretending to ignore it, they

all brushed lightly against one another as they moved through the crowd—eager, excited, and probably a little anxious too. In their bright red-and-black uniforms, they were linked together and looked like a team.

How far they had come as a team we would find out later in the day.

A tournament organizer informed me that we would be playing on the main field, just before the start of the men's championship soccer game.

"There will be a big audience because of that," he said with a grin. "More excitement for your girls' match, don't you think?"

I smiled and agreed.

More pressure too.

Since there was some time before our game, we headed toward the game field for practice. The girls' coach, Ali Zaka, a local Afghan-American, sent them to jog a few laps for a warm-up, then started them dribbling the ball around the field.

On the other side, the girls on the opposing team were practicing too.

The players stole quick, nervous looks.

Then Samira put on her goalie gloves and took her position in the net. After observing her quiet, wiry toughness during practices earlier that week, Ali had chosen her for this crucial role.

"She reminds me of a goalie on my team," he told me when I asked him why. "She *seems* like a goalie."

I watched Samira. Ali was right. Her movements were

precise, steady; she was fearless—unafraid to dive to make a save.

Her teammates lined up to take shots on her. Laila's shot was smooth and strong. She could generate a surprising amount of momentum with her kicks, but Samira remained on secure footing, alert and ready.

⟨⊛⟩

TWENTY MINUTES PASSED. The loudspeaker coughed: "The all-girls soccer team from Afghanistan is about to begin an exhibition match with an Afghan-American girls' team. This precedes the men's final on the main field."

The crowd came to life, a mixture of murmurs and shouts greeting the news.

"From Afghanistan?"

"Did the announcer say *girls* from Afghanistan?"

Yes, I thought. *Girls from our homeland.*

Here to play soccer.

Ali blew the whistle. We huddled in the middle of the field.

It was hard for me at this key moment. I couldn't understand what Ali was telling the team. I had come to the United States as a very small child, and English was my strongest language. I spoke and understood Pashto, because my family was from Kandahar. But Dari was the dominant language of Kabul, where the girls were from; it was the language they all had in common. Ali spoke Dari.

I was envious. Waiting for translations put me out of the loop, as though I were watching an out-of-sync movie.

Who would play what position was clear, however. Ali had appointed Robina, fourteen, as a forward. She was fast, her kick sure. Robina had emerged as a natural team leader: first one on the field, last one to leave. She often had the last word, because she didn't compete for airtime. She'd help the younger girls make sense of Ali's coaching.

Ali put Freshta, also fourteen, as the other forward. Her playing style was a cross between courageous and untamed, always at the ready to take the shot but unfocused on where she aimed her kicks. Nonetheless, Freshta's aggressiveness and flair made her a natural scorer.

Ali positioned Ariana, Miriam, and Laila, Freshta's sister, as defenders. At sixteen, Ariana was the oldest and biggest of the girls, and her height and strength made her a protective wall. Laila's unruffled demeanor and quick intelligence enabled her to stay calm in the crises that constantly erupted around the goal, and fourteen-year-old Miriam's steady, careful game was well suited to claiming and defending a small, clear space.

Ali was choosing well. He put the two youngest girls, Nadia, twelve, and Deena, eleven, as midfielders, where they could scamper after the ball wherever it took them.

Roya was Ali's youngest sister; an Afghan-American, she'd joined the Afghan team as the ninth member after the girls arrived in the United States. Ali placed her as an anchor on offense.

"Stay together as a team," he instructed them. "Don't everyone run after the ball. Play hard."

I understood that much of what Ali had said, and hoped that the girls would be able to act on it.

THE GAME WAS being played on a less than full-sized pitch. Still, it was plenty big for these girls. It was a 6 versus 6 tournament, which meant that not all the girls would be on the field at the same time. Soccer is usually played with eleven players on each side, but on the youth and amateur levels that number can be lower.

The six starters—Robina and Freshta as forwards, Ariana and Laila on defense, Roya as midfielder, and, of course, Samira on goal—ran out onto the field as the crowd erupted with cheers.

On the sidelines, Nadia tossed me a grin, her large green eyes like saucers, and Deena bounced up and down as if on a trampoline. Miriam stood at strict attention. We were a little team ourselves.

The whistle blew: The game was on!

I was praying for a close score. Would I be able to reassure or console them if it wasn't close? Pride can be a fragile thing, and the girls' teamwork was still a work-in-progress. If they didn't win, would each girl blame herself, or would they take out their frustrations on one another?

Then it hit me.

I was expecting the girls to lose.

Robina and Freshta penetrated the defenses downfield, whacking shots whenever they drew close to the goal. Freshta launched wild kicks that soared wide and high—right into the goalkeeper's hands. But she shook off each lost shot, unfazed.

Laila, though, frowned over each of Freshta's misses, miffed that her sister's errant play had cost the team a precious goal.

Ariana drifted around her team's net, batting the ball away with almost languid strides. Samira remained focused, waiting to be tested.

Parallel to Ariana on defense was Miriam, who'd been subbed in for Laila. She squinted at her teammates scrambling after the ball. They kept bunching up, instead of spreading out to set up plays toward the goal.

Miriam yelled at them, in Dari, "Pass the ball, pass it to me."

When no one heeded her, Miriam dashed off the field straight toward a startled Ali on the sideline.

"What are you doing? Get back in the game!" he shouted, shooing her back onto the field.

Miriam said something to Ali and then trotted back into position. She was attempting to carry out Ali's instructions, but no one passed to her. Even waving her arms and shouting brought no results. She stood on the left side of the field alone.

I hadn't gotten to know Miriam very well. On the field she was quick to anger. During her flashpoints, though, I thought I saw a softer sadness in her face.

Nadia had also been subbed in. The stress of the game did not much affect her, and her eagerness to start playing was uncomplicated. For Nadia, it was enough just being on the field with her new friends.

She took the game seriously, though. But not quite so seriously as eleven-year-old Deena, the youngest and the smallest of them all, a spunky four feet six inches tall. Off the field everyone thought she looked like a doll, with her sunny personality, oval face, and cute button eyes. When she played soccer, however, she became tenacious, going after every ball and not at all shy about bumping and shoving other players—who were all, inevitably, much bigger than her.

A miniature train in constant motion, Deena's petite body housed a natural athlete. She had gifts that could not be taught: confidence, scrappiness, heart, and an ability to reach the "zone," where nothing exists but the player and the game.

Possession shifted between the teams as each goalie faced shots, saving all of them. After fifteen minutes, the halftime whistle blew, and seconds later a goal was scored on Samira.

It had come after the whistle. Even so, Ali and I spent most of halftime trying to explain why it hadn't counted. The girls were unsettled. They glared at the other team and listened to us skeptically.

Robina and Samira were especially agitated, waving their hands and talking intently to their teammates, who kept their heads down. Again, I couldn't follow their Dari directly, but across the language divide, I felt for Samira. As a goalie it is difficult not to alienate yourself from the team, to feel helpless. You stand alone in your crease, alert to the other team's break past your defenders, aiming their drive directly at you.

Finally Ali and I convinced them: They were still in the game.

The second half began. Samira's hands were up and she balanced on her toes, her goalie gloves tightened to her wrist with Velcro bands. Her body language read, *You're not going to score on me again.*

For some reason I found myself thinking about how meticulously Samira brushed her hair, pulling it back into a ponytail, with every strand in place. This minute attention to detail might serve her well as a goalie.

Samira pointed and shouted directions to her teammates.

"Stay here! Shoot, shoot! I can handle it!"

But I wondered, being so new to the position, if she really could handle the pressure.

The game ended in a draw.

return to kabul

"I have a longing beyond expression to return to Kabul.
How can its delights ever be erased from my heart?"
—KING BABUR, SIXTEENTH CENTURY

 AMIRA EMERGES FROM the plane blinking in the sun. It's early August 2004 and she and the team have just returned from America and landed in Kabul. She is barely aware of her teammates clambering down the metal airplane steps behind her. They gather on the international runway, a stretch of rough open pavement.

Home.

The other passengers trudge off into the distance. Samira is still. Her teammates follow Jennifer, an English teacher from the Afghan Center who met them in Dubai, and now leads them toward the terminal a few hundred feet away.

Samira squints toward the building—a one-story slab of low, stained concrete. A dusty sign, "*Ba Kabul Khush Amadin*," announces in blue swirled print, "Welcome to Kabul." She begins to sweat. The mountains in the distance are shrouded in haze, pocked by the shadows of colorless mud-brick houses crowding their sides.

Less than forty-eight hours ago she was in the Dubai airport—a modern building with air-conditioning, arched hallways festooned with glittering lights, sheer glass walls, and palm trees. There, travelers in tank tops and jeans mingled with women in *hijabs* and men wearing long white robes.

They'd spent the night in a hotel and planned to catch the flight to Kabul the following morning. Halfway to the airport, Freshta had suddenly clapped her hand against her head.

"My medal!"

In the haste of last-minute packing and the excitement about going home, she'd left behind the gold medal that had been awarded to each girl at the Soccer Cup tournament in Virginia. Freshta refused to board the plane without it.

So they'd told the cab to turn around and edged their way back to the hotel through the snarled rush-hour traffic. By the time they made their way back to the airport, the flight had left.

Samira experienced another day away from home like a sack of stones dropped on her chest.

. . .

When they finally boarded the Kam Air plane the next morning, it appeared to Samira like a shard of the Emirates aircraft that had carried them from New York to Dubai.

That huge plane had tiny bathrooms with flushing toilets and faucets that gushed water at the lightest twist. At home, Samira walks to the well for water. A small TV embedded in each seat offered everything from cartoons, to Shakira tracks, to Bollywood films. During their fourteen-hour flight, regular hot meals arrived, of rice, marinated meat, steamed vegetables.

On the last leg of the journey home, Samira stared out the window of the Kam Air plane as it slipped past Kabul's mountain peaks—a jagged, ancient jaw encircling the city. As it lofted over the edges of the mountains, the only color she noticed on the city's dust-brown landscape was the blackened skeletons of bombed out planes rusting along the runways.

Now, standing on that runway, Samira sees the planes up close—their bodies unnaturally askew, wings bent backward like broken elbows.

The team enters the terminal and is ushered into a side room, where an airline worker brings their luggage. Samira gasps. Her three bulging bags are dirty and battered; the zipper has been torn off one, leaving the seam open and ragged. Her clothes spill through the tear, exposing toys for her siblings, jeans, soccer equipment stuffed into every crevice. Someone may have tried to pull things out. Some of the other girls' bags are missing entirely. Samira drags her scuffed, torn suitcases outside into the unpaved parking lot.

Duaine from the Afghan Center has arranged cars to take all the girls home. Samira lives with eight of her siblings and her parents in a three-room mud-brick house near the base of the hills in Kabul's Karte Parwan district. She will travel along with Ariana, who lives on a quiet street in Khayr Khana, and Miriam, whose family lives higher among the rocky hills, in the Old City.

The three girls climb into the Toyota Surf SUV. They pull the doors shut. Samira sits by the window. The seat feels hot against her back, her arms, her upper legs. The air inside the car is dusty. Samira takes in the closed doors, the closed windows. She has trouble breathing.

The car follows the flat stretch of Airport Road into the main city. Samira stares at the city before her.

It is a dense amalgam of thousands of years of conflicting cultures. Some trace Kabul's ancient founding to the feuding brothers Cain and Abel. Shifting alliances and bloodshed would define its history, as civilization after civilization clashed over the city. It was captured and ruled alternately by the Greeks, the Scythians, the Kush, and the Persians. Islam was established in the ninth century. Later came successive invasions of the Mongol, Persian, and British empires.

The melding of peoples produced an eclectic culture, which remained as a collective imprint on the psyche of the city. Many peoples have a home here. All of Afghanistan's predominant ethnicities—Pashtuns, Tajiks, Hazaras, Uzbeks—mix colorfully in the streets: girls with red hair and freckles; blond and blue-eyed children; men with an Asian cast to their features; women with dark skin, black hair, and almond eyes.

This intersection of cultures, high art, extravagant history, continual war, and wretched poverty has given Samira a stunning and chaotic city in which to live.

Samira presses her face against the window. Along the roadside are market stalls with strips of colored fabrics stretched over the tops, covering shelves and barrows heaped with watermelons, lemons, oranges. Lush stacks of vegetables are arranged in bins, the vibrant colors—greens, reds, ginger yellows—startling against the brown dust of the landscape. Carcasses of sheep, sides of beef, only some skinned, dangle across doorways. Still other entries have pictures of Bollywood actresses in their shadows, like Aishwarya Rai draped in a slender, low-cut sari.

As the car continues through traffic, Samira sees an encampment of the nomadic Kuchi tribe. Their enclave of delicate cloth tents, tethered donkeys and cows, and clusters of sheep is built right up against the road. Children play games, chasing one another between the tents. The Kuchis travel with the shifting seasons, and their women are known for their gorgeously colored clothing of emerald, crimson, cerulean.

The car curves around the hustle and bustle of Massoud Circle, named for the Afghan commander assassinated on September 9, 2001. Buses, cars, and armored trucks clog the road. Armed guards and traffic conductors wave their arms to little effect. There are no clear traffic lanes, lights, or markings of any kind. Stationed alongside the slowed-down cars, men hawk cell phone calling cards.

In the Wazir Akbar Khan district, tents give way to sedate streets, universities, schools, and embassies, flags fluttering. Flanking the official buildings are large and spacious homes with elegant patterning carved into the walls.

The car speeds along the outskirts of Shari-now, one of the main centers of town. Rickety multistory buildings radiate around traffic circles. Signs for Alokozay Tea, Afghan Wireless, and Roshan, in Pashto, Dari, and English, are plastered up and down the sides of buildings. Kocha Morgha ("Chicken Street") and Kocha Gol ("Flower Street") brim over with vendors bustling around their open-air stalls.

The road turns to rubble. The girls bounce along into Wazir Abad, heading north on Taimani Road, to Khayr Khana. On many of the homes they pass, the cement slathered on the façades has cracked, revealing ragged rows of stacked clay bricks. Some have battered wood or sheets as doors. In others, entryways open out onto the street.

When they reach her home, Ariana scrambles out of the car, grabs her bags, and waves good-bye. The driver swings back through Shari-now, heading south on Salang Way toward Kohi Asamayi ("TV Hill"), whose sprouting antennas provide signals to all of Kabul.

Miriam jumps from the car when they arrive at her house. "*Khoda hafez*, Samira *jan*," she calls, saying good-bye.

Then the driver heads west on Salang Way, north toward Karte Parwan.

Flocks of sheep are herded down the sidewalks, donkeys wander through alleys, beggars stand in the traffic circles or next to the street sellers. Trash has been heaped against the backs of buildings, along the sides of the roads, and scattered across the dried bed of the Kabul River.

Samira's excitement at returning melts.

As she is taken through the city, the heat and the dust, it is as if she has never seen any of it before.

Why did I have to come back?

The driver leaves Samira at the base of the hill. Her house sits at its summit. She hauls her bags up the steep cement steps and through the first small gate.

She treads up the narrow, dirt path, avoiding the open sewers on both sides.

As she nears the second and final gate, she calls out, "*Madar, Padar*—I am home!"

There is no answer. "Jawed *jan*! Nasima *jan*! I am home," she calls out for her oldest brother and sister.

They rush outside.

"Samira *jan*!"

Nasima flings her arms around Samira, as her brother gathers up her bags.

"Where are our parents?" Samira asks.

"They are at our grandparents'," Nasima says. "We didn't know you'd be arriving today!"

"We didn't even recognize your voice!" Jawed says.

"Can you find them and tell them to come home?" Samira asks, as she turns toward the door of their home. "I miss them."

"No, not here," Jawed says, guiding her away from the house she was just about to enter. "We don't live there anymore."

Jawed steers her to a house across the road.

"This is our new house. We live here now."

"I'll call Uncle," Nasima says, as they reach the doorway of the new home. "He can walk over and tell them you're here."

Samira's grandparents do not have a phone.

She steps into the unfamiliar hallway. Sloping dark walls form a small entryway. She drops her bags and walks tentatively through the new rooms. A half hour later, her parents burst through the doorway.

"You look healthier," her father, Zaki, says at once, approvingly.

"I am happy you are home, Samira *jan*," her mother, Malika, says, giving her a hug. "I have sat on our roof counting the planes since you left, wondering when my dear Samira will return."

A while later, guests—extended family and neighbors—arrive to welcome her back. Samira entertains them for hours.

After the last guest leaves, the euphoria fades. Samira studies her family's new house. It is very dark, darker than their old home. The living room window overlooks a brick wall.

The yard is divided by walls and rocks and is not the broad, open space she loved at their first home.

Here, shadows seem to hover in every room.

FROM THE TIME Samira was five, her family lived across the street from this new house. It too was a three-room mud-brick home: a main room for visitors, a private room for the family, and a third small room their father used for lessons. At night, they unrolled *toshaks*, mats, and slept on the floors. Outside, the children played in a large yard, protected by walls.

Samira's father, Zaki, always involved himself in his children's lives, education, and physical health. Early on, he set their routine. Every morning at sunrise, he would enter the children's room, waking them for *fajr*, the morning prayer.

Before breakfast was exercise. The children trooped outside together. Zaki, short, bull-chested, directed the children to run back and forth in the yard, raise their arms, swivel side to side at the waist, to stretch out muscles in their arms and legs.

The yard seemed endless then to Samira as she pounded after her older sisters. Zaki would yell out encouragement, correcting their form with the same firmness he brought to his job as a police trainer at Kabul Police Academy. "Bend your knees! Keep your head up, hands loose at your sides."

Faces flushed, he and the nine children would come back inside, where the children's mother had prepared a breakfast of milk and naan, or sometimes eggs.

Each afternoon, when he returned from work, Zaki called his children together for lessons. The schedule and topics were taped on the door outside their small lesson room, which had a blackboard nailed to one wall.

The children were separated into two groups, divided by age. Zaki stood at the front of the room and called in each group for their session.

The children filed in, taking their places on *toshaks* along the floor. Each day they covered two subjects, rotating among math, Pashto, Dari, and writing.

Samira and her sisters quizzed one another on these lessons, even as they completed their assigned household chores. They would repeat vocabulary words as they beat the rugs and mats, test each other on the multiplication tables as they swept the rooms. They were eager to impress their father with their intellectual, as well as domestic, achievements, when he arrived back home.

Samira was enrolled in school at age five. She was thrilled to start at Shireeno School, imagining it would be like home— her classmates as sisters, the teacher like her mother.

But when she arrived, she did not know the girls, and the teachers were strangers and not necessarily kind. She cried for the first chaotic day—then slowly made friends.

On her third day, as she chatted with a new friend beside her, the entire classroom went silent. She looked up. The substitute teacher was glaring at her. Samira had clearly been asked a question, but she hadn't heard.

"*Bakhes*," said the teacher. "*Dastita bigee.*"

Stand up. Give me your hand.

Samira stood up, aware that every classmate was watching her. She extended her hand.

The teacher forced her palm toward the floor and struck the back of her hand with a ruler.

The strikes from the ruler felt like scorpion bites, searing pain that flared red across her skin.

"I won't go to school again," Samira told her mother, Malika, that night. "I hate it."

The next day, her mother visited the teacher. The teacher explained: Samira had ignored her, disrespected the lesson, and been unable to answer a simple question in class. After her mother related this to her, Samira felt ashamed.

It was my fault.

She wouldn't let it happen again.

As first grade progressed, Samira came to love the competition with the other girls, loved winning awards for Pashto recitals or penmanship. On Fridays, when there was no school, she felt bored. Even as young as she was, she wanted to learn, to prove herself, to be the head of her class.

Then, after only one year in school, suddenly she was no longer allowed to go. The doors of Shireeno School were locked. All the girls' schools were closed. The Taliban had come to Kabul.

And Samira's life changed.

Her parents had always encouraged her and her sisters to believe that they could become whatever they dreamed of being. But now it seemed women were no longer allowed to get a job, go to school, study at home, or even laugh in public.

Samira's short-haired, trouser-wearing tomboy older sister, Fatima, who won all the races in their backyard, had always vowed to become an engineer. But she was hastily married to a boy from the best family her father could find. Taliban guards had been taking young women and wedding them to suitors of the Taliban's choice.

The police force had been disbanded and Samira's father was not able to work. He spent his days at home, joining her mother in the kitchen, where they cooked together side by side.

Samira's brother Jawed had always walked Samira and her sisters to school and escorted them home when classes were done. Now he wrapped his head in a *longi*, a turban, and went to work at a car mechanics shop, the family's only financial support.

Samira's father, though, still shaved every morning, in defiance of Taliban orders. And every day he still gave his children lessons, illegal now for his daughters, in chemistry, mathematics, biology, Dari.

Samira felt like a bird in a cage, trapped inside her three-room house with three sisters, four brothers, and both parents, for weeks, then months, then years. Fatima, now married, lived with her husband's family.

The Taliban had an edict against owning or watching TV. Most families hid their TV and VCR. Even so, Samira and her siblings sometimes watched at night, defying the Taliban and the warning of their father. Samira's favorite movie was *Snow White*—in which a beautiful girl was betrayed by someone she trusts. She lay preserved in a glass case, seemingly dead, her body guarded by her small friends, until Samira's favorite part, when she was brought back to life by the kiss of her prince.

Everyone, it seemed, was bolder at night. Samira's father slipped into the shadowed Kabul streets to visit relatives across the city, staying on side streets to avoid being snared by patrols. The Taliban had been searching for him, to ask about his work with the former regime.

One evening, Samira, her family, and guests were watching a Bollywood film, with the curtains drawn, and there was a knock on their door.

The music from the movie had been too loud.

The gathering broke apart in panic. If the adult men were found, they would be arrested, or worse. Samira's father, uncle, and great-uncle rushed out of the room. They scrambled up metal stairs in the hallway, pulled themselves onto the roof to hide—leaving only Samira's cousin and elderly grandfather to stay with the women. Samira's aunt grabbed the movies scattered on the floor—remnants of a debate on what to watch—and hid them. Samira and her mother yanked the power cord from the wall and covered the TV with blankets in a weak attempt to hide it. Then they all stood still, not making a sound. Samira met the eyes of her sister, Azita, just a year older. They held their breath, terrified.

"I will go," whispered their grandfather, Mustafa.

He walked to the door, stooping his body slightly. He assumed a kindly expression. He cracked open the door.

"I heard music." The Talib stood in the doorway.

"Maybe you have made a mistake," Mustafa suggested in a gentle manner, his voice wavering slightly.

All the Talib saw was an old man, alone in the hallway. The house was silent.

With a sour glance inside, he left.

One morning, in October 2001, when Samira was ten, she begged Jawed to take her with him to the market. As they walked the dirt road, Samira lifted her face to the sunlight, feeling its fading warmth. The streets were empty.

Ahead of them on the street, there was a car with two Talibs in it; both children tensed. Suddenly, two men approached the car. They reached in and dragged the Talibs out. The men slammed the Talibs' heads against the hood of the car, punching and pounding them. More men poured out of the surrounding houses and streets, holding guns and firing them in the air, explosions of noise and smoke. Samira and Jawed grabbed hands and ran home.

Samira's uncle confirmed that it was official: The Taliban had been routed.

IN THE AFTERMATH of the Taliban's departure from Kabul, Samira's father rejoined the Police Academy and continued his regimen of physical education for his children. Samira was enrolled again in school, in the second grade, and her eldest sister set her sights on college.

Samira hoped to become a surgeon. As soon as TV was regained, she watched TV surgeries, thinking that it would help prepare her for medical school.

In the spring of 2004, Samira was approached by her teacher, who knew of her interest in sports. "Would you like to join a soccer team? And perhaps compete in America?" Samira nodded. "I'll speak with my parents, but yes!"

Malika was glad to foster her daughter's independence. Samira's father, Zaki, also approved.

But her aunts, cousins, uncles, and neighbors were not as thrilled. The family was confronted at family gatherings, while browsing for vegetables in the markets, or picking out clothes in open-air stalls.

How could they let their young daughter travel without them—for soccer?

"We know what to do," Malika and Zaki told them. "It's our own life."

come back, come back

SAMIRA, KABUL

"The demands on the goalie are mostly mental; for a goalie, the biggest enemy is himself. Not a [ball] not an opponent, not a quirk of size or style."
—KEN DRYDEN, NATIONAL HOCKEY LEAGUE
HALL OF FAME GOALTENDER

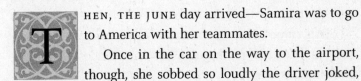HEN, THE JUNE day arrived—Samira was to go to America with her teammates.

Once in the car on the way to the airport, though, she sobbed so loudly the driver joked, "Is she a baby that she cries so much after her mom?"

Robina was sitting next to her. "Why are you crying?"

"What if we go and they don't let us come back?"

Robina tried not to smile.

"No," she said gently. "Why would they do that?"

. . .

But when they arrived in the U.S., Samira was bolder.

While training in Washington, D.C., she attracted the notice of their coach, Ali Zaka. Her intensity and daring nature, her ability to stand alone, were well suited to the lonely task of goalie.

She settled into the net before games, tugging on her gloves, intent on the field. She'd imagine each game within her control—and only hers. That felt good. She liked the responsibility, wasn't intimidated. She felt the weight of it. If she stopped the shots, her team couldn't lose. Then there were the few moments when the opposing players would drive downfield, barrel past Laila or Miriam on defense, and blast the ball toward her. The terror she felt was exhilarating—the opponents seemed to fly toward her, eyes narrowed as they launched the ball at her body—but equally exhilarating was how she could swat it away.

One muggy June afternoon, the game was going badly. It was the Afghan team's second game in the States, and Samira stood tensely in the goal. Her teammates ran around the field after the ball like bees in a swarm.

Shots came to her, one after the other. Most of them she stopped, but a few got through. Her team had lost their discipline, their strategy.

I have to go in.

She had convinced herself that she could save the game—score a goal. She pulled off her gloves and threw them on the ground. She ran forward. The goal was left empty.

Her teammates were confused. They were still learning

the rules of soccer: Was Samira allowed to leave the net? Perhaps it was a new rule?

Their coach, however, was frantic. He hurried toward Samira, signaling her with his hands, *back, back*. "You are the goalie! You have to go in the goal," he said loudly in English.

Samira understood. But she wouldn't go back. With the game still in reach, she had to be in it. She couldn't stand there at the net, alone and helpless. She waved him off.

Now her teammates joined in the chorus: "Go back, go back," they yelled. Reluctantly, she trotted back to the net. Luckily no goals were scored on them while she was on the field.

But they lost the game.

She was very quiet after the loss. But there were thoughts buzzing in her head.

That wasn't Samira's only moment as a field player. During warm-ups in Cleveland, before the International Children's Games, Laila lofted a long, hard shot that slammed against the tip of Samira's finger, snapping it back. Her finger swelled and was wrapped in stiff gauze and ice. Freshta volunteered to step into goal, as Samira hovered anxiously on the sidelines.

They were playing El Salvador, a team of skilled girls who muscled the ball past the Afghan defenders. Shot after shot slipped past Freshta's inexperienced lunges.

Then Robina fell. She and an El Salvador player had collided. Robina limped off the field, clutching her knee.

"I will deal with this," Samira told her teammates.

"Put me in," she asked their coach, Ali Kazemaini.

"Okay," Ali said.

Samira strode onto the field.

"Stay in goal," she yelled to Freshta.

The play resumed. Samira made a beeline for the El Salvadoran player and plowed into her, kicking forward, knocking them both to the ground.

The other girl slowly stood up, her face bleeding.

Samira scrambled up as her teammates clustered around her.

"Are you okay?" Ariana asked her.

"I'm fine. I'm perfect."

"Why did you do that?"

"They kicked Robina!"

Samira earned a new nickname: "The Dangerous One."

Only four days later, as they boarded the plane back to Dubai, Samira chattered excitedly with her teammates—they were going to see their families again, their friends, their homes. She laughed at her old fear, that they might not let her come back.

Until they landed in Afghanistan, she never thought that the person who wouldn't let her "come back" would be her.

NOW SAMIRA IS home.

She grew used to the noise of America, the shrieks of laughter from the team's meals together, the coaches' yells as they drilled on the practice fields, Nadia's quips and raspy laugh, Freshta's bossy voice, Ariana's soothing, mildly sarcastic promises to sort out conflicts, Miriam's indignant shouts when teased, and even Robina's weeping when they did not win.

In America, her head was filled with voices, continuing conversations. Now there is silence.

She remembers each day being packed more tightly than her suitcase.

There, each morning she woke up eager to find out what would happen next. Here, she lies on her *toshak* on the floor and stares at the cracks splintering across the ceiling. Samira eats what is put in front of her, cleans what she has been told to clean, leaves for school, walks back home. She doesn't remember the lessons. She avoids the TV room, where the family congregates.

She sits by herself in the dark. The light from the sky filters through the window, then slowly fades. The walls loom above her, full of shadows. The room is very black. Days are very tiring.

Samira has come back home. But the country she clung to while she was away is gone.

And the time in the United States feels like something she imagined, like a dream.

I want to go back.

Malika recognizes what is happening to Samira. She knows what it is like to live in a memory.

Samira is not the only family member to have lost daily swims in a beautiful pool surrounded by flowers. Her mother had such a pool outside her two-story home back in Guldara.

Malika still misses her childhood home and its garden, her father returning from his work in Kabul every Thursday afternoon, in a dark suit and neatly knotted tie, hair cleanly parted and brushed back, his arms full of fruit from the Kabul bazaar.

Everything was destroyed by the war.

SAMIRA HAS GATHERED things she collected in the U.S.—a doll, her soccer uniform, her cap, a sports bag. Each item has a story. So does each photograph, torn museum or game ticket, her medal and certificate. She arranges them carefully in a box. Every day, she pulls the box out and lays each piece on the floor, her mind reliving where she got it, who gave it to her, where she was, how she got there. After touching each object, she carefully replaces them all in the box and puts it away.

Her family hovers, unsure of what to do. Her mother asks, "Where did you stay? What did you do? What did you eat?"

Jawed wants to know about America. "What was it like? How were the people? How are they different from Afghans?"

Nasima asks, "Did all the girls have their own room?"

They gather around her, pelting her with questions that sting like small, hard stones.

"*Chup bash,*" she says softly to herself, when they ask. Be quiet. Their questioning makes her head hurt.

"Let her be," her father says when he sees Samira shrugging, murmuring her responses. "She just got back. Let her relax."

He and Malika worry. Perhaps there is a way for her to reconnect with Afghanistan while still keeping her memories of America alive.

Malika enrolls Samira in an English course, along with her sister Nasima, so she will not be alone.

It does not work. During class, thoughts slip inside Samira's mind, blotting out the teacher as she drones "desk, house, chair." Samira is desperate to go home, back to her box, to the objects filled with memories.

Once a diligent student, now she closes her book, staring into space, not speaking, sometimes for hours.

Her mother enters the small room where Samira has secluded herself. A slant of light cuts across the faded carpet.

"Che feker mekhuneed?" her mom asks her. What are you thinking about?

Samira ducks her head.

"Khandan," her mother implores her. *Study.*

Samira knows her mother is right. She tries. But she can't. *Come back come back come back,* she says to her mind. But her mind wanders, and it gets lost.

Like an ache in the back of her mind, she loves her family deeply, longs to leap across the distance that has been growing. *But how?*

One afternoon, her family leaves for a visit. Samira doesn't ask where they are going. She is left alone in the house. She opens her album; one picture, and suddenly she can taste the cold, thick sweetness of the ice cream she ate with Ariana one morning in America.

She picks through the photos on every page. As she relives each moment from the trip, the days blur together, forming one long, unbroken memory.

Like bubbles in her mind, memories float like a dream. She and her teammates board a boat that sinks beneath water, then is launched into a fire.

The boat carries them through dark caverns with scary forms screaming, reaching out long, sharpened fingers to swipe at the boat as they float by. Two giants wielding sticks appear, trying to make them crash. Fire erupts and they fall, plummeting into darkness, plunging back into the water.

It was a ride Samira and the girls went on. She leapt out when it was done; Laila and Freshta rode again and again.

In her mind, her dream, her lost space, she and her teammates arrive at a theater. They lean back in cushioned chairs as the movie, hundreds of feet high, begins to play— only somehow they slip behind the screen and become part of it. Wearing blue and red glasses, they shrink back as a fairy flies forward and gathers them all into a carriage. Their seats shake as the carriage rattles over uneven ground. The carriage brings them to the house of a witch, who lunges forward, raising her arms, summoning her magic. Samira screams. Dozens of small mice dart between their chairs, brushing past their feet. Then the lights come on. There is nothing there.

In the world of her mind, Samira and her teammates board a train that rises *up up up,* carrying her with it, soaring into the sky. She looks down, and thinks to herself, *I might not come back alive.*

Now, in her room in Kabul, Samira holds her head in her hands: *What is happening to me?*

So many bubbles in her mind. The chasm between her and her family widens.

There are days when she feels sick with longing. She calls Freshta and the other girls and asks: "What are you doing?"

She begs Freshta to send her a tape they listened to in the U.S., the song "Hug me, Hug me, Kiss me, Kiss me."

She lives for Fridays.

The team has continued to practice soccer in Afghanistan. Every Friday morning, they gather at the Roots of Peace office—a small, grassy compound with a little rose garden inside its tall stone walls. While the team was in the U.S., Duaine took a position with the nongovernmental organization (NGO) Roots of Peace, and their offices were now the site of the team's weekly practice sessions.

Each week they scrimmage for hours, breaking only for a lunch of rice and slices of *tarbuz,* watermelon.

As Samira stands in goal, her thoughts surround her, spirit her mind away. Then the opponents score.

"They just made a goal on you!" Ariana shouts at her, glaring.

"I'm okay," Samira says, shaken, angry at herself. "I will focus. I can handle it."

THEN IT BECOMES clear that her withdrawal may begin costing more than games.

There is a girl in her neighborhood. At first she was only very quiet. Then she started spending time alone in a room, then wandering by herself in the streets. Now she rambles, mumbles nonsense. People avoid her in the street.

Samira is scared.

That could be me.

. . .

Fear gives her new focus. It has been two months since Samira returned to Afghanistan—she must find a way out of her downward spiral.

She thinks of all the times she was determined to do something, and then just went ahead and did it. That is how she will reclaim her life. She becomes a goalie of her mind, blocking each thought before it can penetrate, deflecting each memory with a sharp counterimage.

When thoughts gather in her mind, she grabs the bright yellow ball given to her in the States and invites Nasima to play volleyball with her in their small yard.

When her mind starts reconstructing game sequences from Cleveland, she forces herself to remember plot summaries from a story she's reading or a movie she just saw.

When she thinks about the places she visited or the people she met in America, she reminds herself of people she met yesterday.

She finds she can focus on her studies again. At practice she stands in goal, alone at the net, but very much part of the game.

In this way, Samira begins to reenter her life.

nice kick, bad aim

AMERICA, JUNE 2004

T WAS ONE of those can't-breathe-muggy summer days. I paced in my parents' Connecticut living room; I couldn't stay still. Eight months had lapsed since I had begun my project: the Afghan Youth Sports Exchange (AYSE).

And any minute now eight Afghan girls were due to land at JFK Airport in New York City.

I was expecting a call from Barbara Goodno, an American who was accompanying the girls from Afghanistan. Her husband, Duaine, also an American, was the program director for the Afghan Center, an NGO in Kabul. When I'd approached him about the idea of bringing Afghan girls to the States to teach them soccer, he was enthusiastic, and helpful.

Finally, Barbara phoned.

"We're here," she said wearily. "We're all here."

IT WOULD BE another week before I could leave to meet the girls. As they settled into the Goodno home in Potomac, Maryland, I stayed with my parents, helping my mother prepare for the *khatum,* a ceremony in Islam to honor the deceased—in this case my grandmother, my mother's mother, who'd passed away the previous year.

Qamar *jan* had returned to Afghanistan after the fall of the Taliban. But her high blood pressure, manageable in America, had been too much for Afghanistan's decimated medical system. She died less than three months after her return.

We'd invited family and friends to share the *khatum.* That our gathering coincided with the visit by the Afghan girls felt somehow right. I'd lost my grandmother; perhaps I might find some of her in these girls.

All during the week of preparation, I helped my mother cook for our numerous guests. Periodically, I would go to one of the bedrooms, close the door, and telephone Barbara to get an update on the girls' visit.

It seemed she was keeping them busy and entertained.

"They're enjoying our swimming pool," Barbara said, all cheery.

"Wonderful."

"And we took them shopping!"

Another phone call later in the week revealed a visit to the dentist.

"We had a long day," Barbara sighed. "All the girls got fillings. Dr. Rayek was wonderful. His wife and daughter were there to talk to 'the patients.'"

"I hope there were no root canals!" I laughed.

"Well, as a matter of fact, Samira did have one."

Dr. Riaz Rayek was an Afghan-American living in the area who had donated his services completely free of charge.

The last day of the *khatum,* I knelt in our basement, pouring steaming *chay* into an endless line of teacups. The men were upstairs—downstairs, women. Women were everywhere: on the low maroon couches circling the edge of the room, on the thin, dark carpet, and cross-legged on narrow, cushioned sitting mats blanketing the floor. A large white sheet was spread in the center of the floor, to provide a clean surface. Hundreds of pale blue *taspas,* prayer beads, were scattered in small piles around the sheet. They were used to keep track of the number of prayers said, much as a rosary might. The women of our family, their hair covered with pale scarves intricately embroidered with silk thread, and some with tiny mirrors, crowded into the packed room, onto the stairs, and into the hallway above. Part of doing the *khatum* is the collective reciting of the entire Qur'an. The chant of the verses in Arabic rose and fell as voices in prayer filled the house.

At 1 A.M., I edged up to my mother.

"Do you still need my help?" I asked.

"No, you can go to sleep."

Seven hours later, I stumbled out of bed, dressed, loaded my suitcases into my car trunk, along with boxes filled with clothes for the girls, and began the six-hour drive from Connecticut to Maryland.

I was finally going to meet the girls. I was nervous. But, oddly, also calm. I was trying to memorize their names.

I drove with the air-conditioning on full blast, the radio off, leaning forward as if I could get there before the car did.

The night before, I had pored over the photos of the girls Duaine had sent me via e-mail. Would I recognize who was who? What would I say? And how would I say it?

At 3 P.M. I arrived at the Goodno house just off River Road near Washington, D.C., and drove the long, winding driveway, hidden among huge oaks and draping willows. I got out of the car and studied the sprawling, three-story brick house, a shimmer of blue from the pool catching my eye. Barbara had said to enter the house through the open garage door on the basement level. I did.

Quietly, I made my way up the first flight of stairs, into the kitchen and living room areas. Still, no girls—the house was eerily without sound.

"Hello?" I squeaked.

Barbara's flat, Midwestern voice answered from above, "Awista! We're up on the third floor."

I climbed the next flight. Two girls stood at the top of the stairs.

"Salaam," I said, hugging and kissing each one, right cheek first, then left, then right again. They returned the traditional greeting while their eyes darted to my bare legs. I hadn't thought about modesty when I'd dressed in shorts for the heat that morning.

I blew it, I thought, mentally kicking myself. *Now what will they think of me?*

In Afghanistan, and among Afghans in general, modesty is an important ingredient of the culture. In different eras it's been interpreted with different norms.

But my shorts . . .

"My goodness, how nice to meet you at last!" Barbara said as she came to the head of the stairs. We'd been talking all week, but had never met. She was my height, five-three, pale, with red cheeks and a narrow nose. Her gaze seemed unruffled and amused.

She was wearing long pants.

Barbara turned to one of the girls. "This is Nadia."

Nadia's eyes were shockingly green. They reminded me of the young Afghan girl who had graced the cover of *National Geographic* in 1985 with her stunning and haunted look. Nadia caught me staring and looked down. I glanced away. I didn't want to embarrass her.

"And this is Samira," Barbara said in softly spoken English.

Samira smiled, giving me a peek at her perfectly white teeth before shyly covering her mouth with her hand. The dentist had done a nice job, I mused. Samira's light brown hair had been parted neatly on the left and pulled into a tight ponytail. She was slender and graceful in her large, loose T-shirt and dungarees.

I greeted her with the familiar greeting, *"Salaam."*

Barbara led me down the hall to a crowded bedroom filled with suitcases, duffel bags, and four more girls.

"This is Freshta, Laila, Miriam, and Deena," Barbara said, swinging her arm to include all of them.

It was obvious immediately that Freshta and Laila were sisters. I found it hard to tell them apart. Both had long, glossy black hair, a dotting of freckles across their noses, and similar height and build. It would take me a week, but by then I'd wonder how I ever confused them, their personalities were so different.

Barbara turned to the thin girl on her left. "And this is Miriam."

"*Salaam,*" I said.

"*Alaykom assalam,*" she replied in a singsong voice.

Miriam's hair was a deep chestnut color and was loose around her broad, flat face. A scar zigzagged on the left side of her nose. But when she smiled, bright and lovely, the scar disappeared.

Barbara gently pulled another girl forward. Deena was, I knew, the youngest of the group, and she appeared very shy. But Deena's sweet look hid a fighting spirit.

The girls were split between two bedrooms, each with a king-sized bed that, remarkably, was able to sleep four of them.

As we smiled, gestured, and nodded, the last two girls, Ariana and Robina, arrived loaded with bags, fresh from a trip to the mall, along with Barbara's daughter-in-law.

At sixteen, Ariana was statuesque, her brown hair in a single braid down her back. Robina seemed just a bit younger and was short and slight, her posture arrowlike, with olive skin and dark hair, parted down the center. She wore a sporty headband.

Opposites attracted. Ariana and Robina stood holding

hands, smiling at me and then at each other. The two of them somehow matched, like two candles burning at different levels.

After our brief hellos, I went into the extra guest room to change my clothes. We were going to the house of Roya Zaka, a thirteen-year-old Afghan-American girl living in Virginia, whose brother Ali I'd met months earlier.

It turned out that the entire Zaka family were soccer enthusiasts, and they had all thrown themselves into my project. Ali had agreed to coach the girls in the upcoming Afghan-American tournament in Washington, D.C. His uncle Jawed Sanie volunteered to run the first few practices—and, at Ali's urging, his parents agreed to let Roya join the camp.

Coincidentally, it was Roya's birthday. We would bring her back to Barbara's house that evening to be the ninth girl on the team.

Roya would turn out to be pivotal, as both my translator and as a cultural bridge to her young Afghan teammates. In turn, Roya would have the pleasure of meeting girls her own age who still lived in Afghanistan. For this reason too, her family was glad to have her join the team.

Four girls rode in Barbara's car. She would lead the way because her silver Infiniti SUV had a GPS device. I would chug along behind her in my Civic, filled to the brim with the rest of the girls.

I was quiet during the drive. I tried out my rusty Pashto

with Deena and Nadia. The girls were polite, although I must have sounded like a child. Mercifully, after about fifteen minutes they fell asleep in the car. Something they'd repeat every car ride, much to my relief.

∾⟨❊⟩∾

WE ARRIVED AT the Zaka home an hour later. Roya, her brother, her sister, her sister's husband, an uncle, and her mother and father were outside to greet us. Roya was tall, with ebony eyes and eyebrows, and a photogenic smile.

After a slew of "Salaam"s the girls politely lined up at the entrance, each taking her turn to give the customary three-kiss greeting.

We entered the house single file, removing our shoes at the doorway, and were ushered into an ample living room with Afghan furniture. In pairs, the girls crowded together on the low-to-the-ground chairs spread around the room. The carved chairs were dark mahogany, with cushions covered by lushly woven Afghan carpets.

I sat on the sofa with Barbara and Roya's sister, Mariam, who translated for me. At first, the eight girls kept their eyes glued to the living room rug, only looking up and speaking when spoken to.

"Is there anything you need?" Roya's father asked. "Please do not hesitate to ask."

Silence.

"We need prayer rugs, *Kaka jan*," replied Samira, tentatively.

"Ah, yes."

Mariam's husband heard the request and, unbeknownst

to the group, that evening went to a local Afghan market and brought back eight beautifully woven prayer rugs. This was the kind of generosity the girls and the program were met with almost everywhere.

After dinner—the girls' first home-cooked Afghan meal in the U.S.—Ali suggested a game of soccer in the backyard. Everyone brightened.

Roya led us into the spacious yard. On the back porch, facing the yard, Mr. and Mrs. Zaka, Barbara, Roya's uncle, and I settled in to watch them play.

As the game began in earnest, I had a chance to observe them:

Ariana yelled out commands—where to stand, whom to pass to. Robina ran hard and fought for the ball.

Freshta was excitable, loudly encouraging the girls to "Kick, kick" or "Pass the ball! Pass the ball!" Her sister Laila, on the other hand, was quiet but had a kick that sent the ball flying into the neighbor's yard.

"Nice kick, bad aim," roared Roya, which made everyone giggle.

The younger girls, Miriam, Nadia, and Deena, ran around ducking in between the other players, their eyes vigilant on the ball.

Samira had an internal steadiness, a support the team could use. I could almost see her thinking, planning her moves, positioning herself to be open for a pass.

Were these the same girls who had just sat so quietly in the living room?

They continued to play until it was so late we could barely

see. After prying them off the yard, we said our good-byes and drove back to Barbara's, my car quiet with sleeping girls.

Later, as I headed to my room in Barbara's house, I breathed a sigh of relief.

They're here.

As I got ready for bed, it dawned on me that this was the farthest these girls had traveled. I understood that Freshta and Laila had been refugees in Pakistan, but none of the other girls had been outside Afghanistan.

Every night for weeks before they came, I had startled out of sleep, my jaw locked in place. I'd never been so anxious in my life. I was to be responsible for the lives of eight young girls (nine, including Roya) for six weeks—not only as a program manager, but also as a kind of mother figure half a world away from their home.

And in this, I would be largely alone. A rotating series of family, coaches, colleagues, and friends would cycle in and out, but I'd be the only constant.

Here I was, a twenty-something woman, used to going for a run in the morning, a latte in the afternoon, and a movie whenever I felt like it. Now I was thrust—or rather I had thrust myself—into a role that would demand all my time and energy: an overnight "soccer mom."

What if some emergency happened? I couldn't speak Dari, and my Pashto was poor. I could organize each hour of each day. I could make sure the girls developed their athletic skills. I could find, as had happened that evening, ways for them to have fun. But could I help them where they might need it the most, to meet the challenge of being in an entirely new culture?

And inside all this, I had my own cultural divide to cross, an invisible sideline from which I paced.

I knew when I started the project that this would be a large undertaking, yet the enormity didn't sink in until the girls arrived. Was I really up for this?

Well, an inner voice replied, *it's a little late to wonder, isn't it?*

At that, I fell asleep.

෫෫*෫

I WOKE THE next morning in an unfamiliar room. Had last night been a dream? Our first meeting, the hugs, the voices chattering in Dari, Laila's kick soaring over into the neighbor's yard?

In jeans and a T-shirt, my hair still wet from the shower, I padded down the stairs to the kitchen, expecting to start breakfast for the girls. Instead, I heard dishes clattering softly against the counter; someone had arrived before me. I turned the corner and saw Robina.

The table was already set with a plate, a cup, and silverware for each girl. Robina was preparing warm milk in the microwave, confidently pushing Time and Start. I gestured, pointing to her and then to me, to the dishes and the microwave, but she motioned for me to sit.

Robina seemed comfortable in her role. Here—and in Kabul too I would find out—she was seen as someone who took care of others.

She set a cup of warm milk in front of me and from behind her back brought out a hidden sugar bowl. With a sly smirk she placed it on the table. She leaned over and touched my hand. "Drink!" she said in Dari.

Barbara had forbidden the girls sugar in an effort to instill what she thought were "healthy habits." A common morning drink in Afghanistan, however, was warmed milk with sugar. Salt was also on Barbara's no-no list.

The girls of course hadn't known about this. The night before, Roya had inquired about their stay at Barbara's. "How is it?" she asked.

"We can't have salt or sugar!" they answered in unison.

Upon discovering this, Mrs. Zaka had placed, in addition to clothes and toiletries, a bag of salt in Roya's suitcase.

The rest of the girls made their way downstairs. The kitchen stirred alive as they moved the chairs and sat at the table. They joked with one another as they reached for the biscuits Barbara had baked for them before she left for work. They quickly drained their warmed milk.

"Sugar!" they exclaimed in Dari. Roya gave them a mischievous smile. I laughed. With Barbara gone, they managed to find the sugar bowl in the cupboard.

Just as quickly, the girls cleaned up. Each one had a task. One cleared the table, another swept up crumbs, another loaded the dishwasher. Like clockwork they completed their assignments. Robina oversaw it all, reminding them what else needed be done, inspecting their work and making sure it was up to par. Once she gave the final check, they were free to leave the kitchen.

Just like a family.

Robina looked around the kitchen once more, checking to see if everything was in its rightful place. She turned toward me and smiled. Her quiet authority and sincere heart reminded me of my best hopes for myself.

that i may play soccer

ROBINA, KABUL, SEPTEMBER 2005

"To Allah belongs the east and the west; wherever you turn, there is the face of Allah."
—QUR'AN 2:115

IN KABUL, ON Friday morning, Robina wakes before dawn, as always. In the shadows before the sun rises, she prepares herself for *fajr*, morning prayer, as the *Azan* echoes across the city.

She rolls her sleeping mat and stores it in the corner, careful to avoid the sleeping bodies of her seven brothers, four sisters, and her father especially. Her mother will be awake soon.

Quietly, she sweeps away dust that sifted overnight from the flaking mud walls to the floor. She changes into loose pants and a long-sleeved shirt, then spreads out a small patterned prayer rug. Dabbing her hands, arms, and face with water left from the previous day, she performs *wudu*—the ritual ablution. She smooths back her long, black hair and tucks it underneath the twist of a head scarf.

By now the sun has lifted into the sky. Back erect, head bowed, feet slightly apart, she faces east, toward Mecca. Palms against her chest, she begins *namaz,* prayer. She lowers herself to the ground, kneeling on the prayer rug, touching her forehead, nose, and palms to the ground. Rising and lowering herself with each *rak'a,* prayer cycle, she ends kneeling. Sitting on the backs of her feet, in silence she makes *du'a:*

> *Insh'Allah* that everyone may enjoy peace and health.
> *Insh'Allah* that I will be safe when I leave my house.
> *Insh'Allah* that I may go to school.
> *Insh'Allah* that I may play soccer.
> *Amin.*

THE ROOTS OF PEACE compound is located in Karte Char, on the southwest edge of Kabul. The roads are wider and quieter there, the buildings more sparse than in Robina's neighborhood of Wasilibad.

At her touch, the compound's large green doors swing open, and she catches the sweet smell of the secluded garden within. Then she slips inside.

Inside the walls, everything is quiet and peaceful, the air fresh and scented with flowers. Even though summer's warmth has cooled, grass still blankets the Roots of Peace field, a saturation of green in the parched landscape. Roses, sunflowers, and daisies are dotted around a small stone office building flanking the field. The light concrete walls rimming the entire complex are delicately carved. They rise high enough to block the noise from the street and prevent outsiders from peering in, but stop short of preventing the occasional overexuberant shot from flying over the wall.

It is September 2005. Robina hurries across the field and drops her bag at the base of the stone wall. She pulls off her head scarf and replaces it with a baseball cap, which she twists backward. She tugs off her sandals and slides into cleats. She pushes up the sleeves of her heavy sweatshirt and trots onto the neatly trimmed field, clapping her hands.

"Let's play," she calls out.

⟨⑤✷③⟩

SHE AND HER teammates have been meeting every Friday since they returned from America a year ago—with two conspicuous absences. The two youngest girls have fallen away: Nadia and Deena, the smallest of them. No one knows precisely what happened. Did their parents pull them out? Is Deena focusing on her studies? Perhaps Nadia and her family moved?

It is common now in Afghanistan for people to disappear without explanation. Despite the "official" end of the war more than three years before, there is still a sense of displacement—families lose their jobs, cancel their cell phones, move away.

Friday is *Jummah*, the holy day in Islam. Schools close and businesses shut down, emptying the streets of the city. Families take trips to Qargha, a lake on the outskirts of Kabul, where they picnic on freshly grilled kebobs and salads, paddle boats, or swim in the lake. Some travel all the way from Kabul to Paghman, a lush district at the base of the Hindu Kush, replete with chalets, waterfalls, and rivers. Others return to their ancestral villages or spend a quiet day at home.

The six remaining girls choose to spend their day differently. Week after week they return to the Roots of Peace field, arriving in the morning to play for hours, until it is time for lunch—piles of glistening *palaw* and bowls of sliced watermelon served at a long folding table inside. Afterward, they rush back outside and race across the field, laughing and shouting, diving after the ball and blasting it past one another's outstretched bodies until it is time to go home.

When the team returned from America the previous August, the difference in their playing was obvious. Before the trip, Robina had had only the most rudimentary knowledge of the game. Although Duaine had organized weekly practices, along with English and computer lessons, they had not received formal coaching. She and her teammates had made up their own rules. They dashed across the field oblivious to any strategy or skill. Then Robina, impatient at the pace of dribbling, would snatch the ball in her hands, run toward the goal, and drop it at the net.

Now, after playing seriously for months, Robina is aware of her body in a new way. Before, it was her hands that were necessary to her: to carry water up the mountain to their house, to scrub the floors, or to write out her lessons. But in soccer, they are useless. Now she's discovered her legs, her balance, the speed with which she can run. And her fore-head, which she uses to butt the ball.

Before soccer, her legs and feet simply got her places, or kicked at rubbish or stones in her way. Now she knows each part of her foot intimately, the way it curves on one side, perfectly contoured to the side of the ball. She knows the strength of the broad, smooth sweep leading up to her ankles, and the dense, solid circle of her heel, perfect for pivoting.

Since their training in America, the game has been trans-formed for Robina. Rather than acting from a narrow, indi-vidual perspective, she feels herself to be part of a team. With twelve eyes working instead of two, they fly across the field in concert, together toward the goal.

❦

WHEN ROBINA WAS a young girl, her mother would send her on errands for the household. She lived on the ground floor of her uncle's two-story home in Qalee Fatullah, with her parents and eleven siblings.

Leaving home, she would pass a small cemetery with its shards of gravestones, go past a small clinic staffed by the single doctor who served the neighborhood, then down the dusty Pay Maskan Road, to scrounge for paper for the family to burn, or to bargain for cucumbers and watermelon in the market. Sometimes she was sent with her sister; sometimes alone. On the way to the bazaar, she'd often pass the park in Karte Parwan—a large, sandy stretch where boys gathered to play soccer or pickup volleyball games.

Hovering at the field's edge, she'd watch the boys tearing

back and forth, shouting and laughing, spraying dust as they kicked the ball high or bounced it on their heads. One of the boys was her older brother, Najib. She admired his speed and his deft footwork as he danced past the other players.

But she wouldn't stay long. She knew her mother would worry, wondering whether she had gotten lost or, *Khoda na kuna,* Allah forbid, had been in an accident.

Robina was five when her mother enrolled her in Wazir Akbar Khan School, where she earned top grades, securing first position in her first grade class. A year later, the Taliban took Kabul. School, along with soccer games in the park, ended.

Education for women had been established almost a century before by King Amanullah Khan, who'd assumed the throne in 1919. During his ten-year reign, the king—along with his strong-willed wife, Queen Soraya Tarzi—instituted a broad array of reforms for women, empowering them to choose their marriage partners and making education compulsory for both genders.

Afghanistan's constitution, ratified in 1931, was one of the most progressive in the region, declaring equality for all citizens and enshrining primary education as a universal right. Kabul University admitted women in 1959, ten years before Princeton University became coeducational.

Although Robina missed going to school, most of her life remained unchanged. At six, she was too young to wear a *burqa,* or to be afraid of the Talibs patrolling the streets, with their long beards, *longi*—turbans—and eyes rimmed with *surma,* khol. Her parents continued working, her mother,

Zainab, as a maid in the home of wealthy Afghans, and her father, Omar, at his cobbler's stall in Deh Afghanan.

Robina and her siblings still ventured out across the city, entering printing stores for paper or carpenter shops for left-over wood scraps to burn in their oven. They still scoured the sidewalks for leaves and branches. They went to playgrounds and parks, where they could push one another on swings or shimmy down slides.

When the Talibs appeared, older children and adults ran to the mosque—vanished from the streets, from the parks, from the boys' soccer games.

Four years later, when she turned ten, Robina was on one of these scavenging trips in Shari-now with her brother Tariq and her sister Salma. An Afghan man cycled past them, then circled back. He had short black hair and was wearing a traditional *paran tumban,* the long light cotton shirt down to his knees, and baggy pants. He climbed off the bike and approached them.

"*Salaam,* my name is Waleed."

"*Alaykom assalam,*" Tariq answered, cautious.

"You are not in school?" he said, looking at the three children.

Tariq shook his head. So did Robina and Salma.

"If you are ready and willing and you think your family will agree," Waleed said, "I will take you to a center for families who can't afford for their children to go to school. We'll teach you there, and keep you away from the streets.

"We take many children—especially girls—who are in the street collecting paper like you," he continued, "and they study writing and math and learn skills like tailoring and woodworking. Would you like to join?"

Salma spoke up. "Yes. We would. But we need to get permission from our mother."

He wrote their names on a list, and their address.

"I'll come to your house to meet with your family, and ask their permission."

Waleed kept his word and showed up a few days later. He explained to Robina's parents that he taught Dari and the Qur'an at *Aschiana,* the Nest. Because they taught the Qur'an, as well as other subjects, *Aschiana* was allowed by the Taliban to continue.

Founded in 1995 by an Afghan engineer, Mohammed Yousef, *Aschiana*'s mission was to empower children who lived or begged on the streets, while still recognizing the economic function they served for their families. Working full-time, the children could earn up to $20 a month, and their families couldn't afford to have them spend all day in school, let alone buy the supplies. Waleed told Robina's parents that the school's sessions were designed in three- to four-hour shifts, either in the morning or afternoon, leaving time for the children to continue earning money the rest of the day. He reiterated that the classes covered the Qur'an, as well as traditional subjects of literacy and math and vocational training. The school also offered practical instruction on health care, land mine awareness, and navigating traffic on foot. There were already three more *Aschiana* centers across Kabul, with two more planned, serving thousands of children.

Zainab listened carefully to Waleed's explanation of the school and its goals.

"It's good for the child and also brings benefits to the family," he continued. "We send each child home with rations of food for everyone."

"Where is the nearest location?" asked Zainab.

"Shari-now."

Zainab thought for a moment. The program sounded promising, but this man was still a stranger.

"Would you take me to the location, so that I can see for myself how it is?"

He agreed. A few days later, Zainab visited the center, a twenty-five-minute walk from the family's house. She saw classrooms full of girls, their heads bent over notebooks or their hands raised to answer questions. Robina, Salma, and Tariq—the children old enough for school, but too young to be working full-time—were enrolled.

Aschiana provided its students with towels, soap, and a toothbrush to wash in the school bathrooms before going to class. The school assigned each student a small locker to store personal hygiene supplies, along with books and notebooks.

Robina continued her trips to find paper and wood. But for a few hours a day, six days a week, she and two of her siblings would walk to the school, clean up, grab their books, and head to the classroom.

Aschiana also provided physical education for all its students, including the girls. For the first time, Robina joined a team—girls' volleyball.

She and her best friend, Tamana, starred on the team, smacking balls past the leaps of other, slighter girls. Tamana lived nearby, and they traveled to school together every morning, studied and practiced together in each other's house. They enrolled in sewing classes and giggled over handmade dolls when they took breaks from studying.

Robina liked her classes in Dari and the Qur'an. When she did well in those subjects, her teachers suggested a class in calligraphy. Her brother joined her, enthusiastically inking curved letters in delicate strokes, while her sister Salma pursued painting classes.

One morning, the Taliban arrived, unannounced. The teachers scrambled to hide older girls in the closets, in the bathroom, or urged them to run home through the back door. The Taliban had decreed that only young girls could be educated, through fourth grade.

A Talib entered Robina's Qur'an class.

The teacher looked squarely at Robina.

"Robina," she said. "Please recite a *surah*."

The Talib watched her, waiting.

Robina could hear the pounding of her heart.

Lowering her eyes, she breathed in, and recited the Throne Verse in Arabic:

In the name of God, the Merciful the Compassionate . . .

Oh, Allah! None have the right to be worshipped but him, the Eternal, the one who sustains and protects all that exists. Neither fatigue, nor sleep overtakes Him. To Him belongs all that is in the heavens and on earth. Who is he that can intercede with Him except with his permission? He alone knows what will happen to his creations in this world, and what will happen to them in the next. They will never be imbibed with any of His knowledge except

that which he wills. His throne arches over the heavens
and the earth. He feels no fatigue in protecting those who
worship him, and He alone is the Most High, the Most
Supreme.

Later, a friend told Robina that the Talib had tears in his eyes at her small, low voice reciting the verse so perfectly. On his way out, he gave the teacher money to support the school.

Soon afterward, though, the Taliban found out that older girls were being taught at *Aschiana*. They arrested the director and imprisoned him, shaving his head to humiliate him. *Aschiana* closed. Still, Robina's teacher would knock at the family's door periodically, bearing baskets with the rations of food that used to be distributed at school.

Robina was not the only child in the family to encounter the Taliban. According to the edict handed down, men were required to grow long beards, but her eldest brother, Najib, now in his early twenties, had been caught in the cross fire of a gunfight during the country's civil war and stabbed by a coworker during a shift in the melon market where he worked. His injuries, especially the gunshot through his jaw, had left him barely able to speak and only able to manage a scraggly fuzz dusting his jaw.

A few years later, as he walked to the market, a Talib stopped him.

"Why is your beard so short?"

He couldn't explain—so they brought him to one of their headquarters, strapped him down, and shaved his head.

A family neighbor witnessed Najib being taken and hurried to Omar's stall.

"They took your son away!" the neighbor shouted.

"Good," Omar mumbled. "It's good the Taliban took him."

Omar announced the news to his family that night. Robina burst into tears. Zainab was stunned; Omar had always been a dour man, and now she realized her husband wouldn't even fight for their son.

She donned her *burqa* and left the house alone. Forcing one foot in front of the next, she walked to the Taliban holding cell closest to where Najib had been seized. Dusk fell, and a black horizon spread over Kabul.

When she arrived at the Taliban headquarters, a Talib was perched on a stool, shaving a succession of heads, as young boys, teenagers, and even older men stood before him. Najib wasn't there. She approached the nearest guard and kept her voice steady.

"My son was just brought here," she said. "He has been very injured in the wars, so please let him go."

His fingers clenched around a long, thin *dura,* a whip that coiled along his side. He raised it over her head.

"Release my son," she asked again. "He has been injured and can't even speak."

He lowered his arms and stared at her.

He gave her the name of another guard. "Release my son," she repeated, and again repeated as she traveled from Talib to Talib, answering question after question.

Hours later, she arrived home with Najib, his scalp raw and scabbed.

Robina and her mother helped her brother onto a mat, so he could lie down.

That night, Robina tossed and turned.

Will our life always be like this? Will it ever change?

WITHOUT *ASCHIANA*, ROBINA continued doing errands for the family. One late afternoon, as usual, she went to refill the large plastic jug with water. She walked the three meters down the road to Baraki, where a public well dispensed water to families throughout the area.

That day, the crowd was particularly large, snaking in a long line down the street. If she waited her turn, she would never get home before dark. So she began knocking on doors of homes, asking if she could use their pump to fill her water jug.

In a house with a blue gate, a young woman opened the door. She smiled pleasantly at Robina.

"Yes," she said. "We have water to share."

They had an actual tap in their courtyard—not a well or a pump—and Robina filled her jug with ease.

"Come back whenever you like," the woman said. "My name is Khadija."

Over the next few days, Robina returned several times. One day, in the yard, a toddler wobbled toward her, arms open, giggling. Robina bent down, smiling.

"*Salaam*, I'm Robina," she said. The child smiled back at her and grasped her fingers.

The boy was the son of Khadija's sister-in-law, Aisha. She also had an even younger son. Her husband worked all day and she was frequently busy with errands or housework. With traditional Afghan hospitality, she invited Robina in for a cup of *chay*.

"Would you be willing to make friends with my children?" she asked Robina, as they sat on couches in the living room. "They're very bored at home."

What Aisha was asking was if Robina could come to live at the house to help take care of her sons. It was not unusual for a wealthier family to invite a young girl into their household to help with chores.

After talking it through with her mother, Robina returned to Khadija's home the next day. She stayed, with brief return visits home, for the next several years.

She enjoyed spending time with the two little boys, Karim and Arian—getting down on the floor to help them build houses out of wooden blocks and tugging them around in small cars with wheels until they squealed in delight. She propped them on her lap and whispered stories as they fell asleep in her arms.

Sometimes the entire family would travel back to their village, trusting Robina alone in the house, where she'd race and slide across the marble floors. And she watched television.

In spite of the Taliban edicts, the family received foreign channels through a satellite dish, and the nightly news broadcast showed clips from soccer games.

It was the first time Robina had seen professional soccer. She was riveted by the stadiums, the stars, the splashy plays and screaming fans from so many countries. She began to search for the games themselves, catching one or two in a row.

Watching soccer began to open her eyes to an experience outside of herself, her daily life in Kabul, her country.

If she yelled out angrily after a bad play, she saw hundreds, if not thousands, of men and women shouting at the same time, their faces twisted in expressions of identical disgust. Or cheering in triumph, scrambling up on the couch pillows and jumping in ecstatic celebration, she'd find herself in sync with an entire stadium half a world away.

She obsessed over the skills of Brazilian star Ronaldinho, his dark ponytail flapping as he swiveled away from a defender's hard swipe.

His feet seemed to fly with the ball. He was smart, remembering a defender's weaknesses or spotting small gaps in the defense, a slit in the tightly woven fabric that was almost invisible until he pushed through it.

Ronaldinho, she believed, was the best player alive.

She imagined herself playing for her own country in a huge stadium, and bringing back a trophy—with Afghanistan's flag, and its athletes, shown on television sets in every country in the world.

Robina felt she was peering through a crack, glimpsing a wild, gorgeous garden outside.

❦

THE NORTHERN ALLIANCE and coalition forces, supported by the United States, drove the Taliban from Kabul the year Robina turned eleven, in 2001. Her mother was given a small television by her employers, and now Robina watched soccer games at home. She discovered fellow enthusiastic fans in her brothers Najib and Tariq, and her sister Salma.

Schools reopened and Robina entered third grade, skipping

second grade thanks to the education she'd received at *Aschiana* before it closed.

She and Tamana rejoined the volleyball team. But soccer had caught her. Soccer was the world's game, and she wanted to be part of it.

She was thrilled to be back in school. Even at eleven, Robina dreamed of becoming a doctor; perhaps she would heal her mother, who'd been weakened by decades of work and childbearing. Such dreams might be possible now.

Family was most important. As much as Robina enjoyed the grandeur of Khadijah's house, she loved going home.

Her family's house was close, just a short walk through the Karte Parwan area, near the Women's Garden, a park reserved for women. Before, under the Taliban, she'd have to hurry down the emptied streets. Once, she saw a bloody hand and leg dangling from a pole. But now she walked free of fear.

At Khadija's, Robina earned small sums of money or small gifts of food and clothes, which she eagerly brought home and presented proudly to her mother.

Then Khadija began to resent these visits home. As a child, Robina had always been welcomed and honored in Khadija's home, as though she were part of the family. As a young woman, she found that that had changed.

She'd always volunteered to help around Khadija's house—enthusiastically sweeping the large rooms with a broom or dusting tables. Dust was everywhere in Kabul.

Over time, she noticed that her help was received less like a generous offer from a guest and more like something expected. If the family needed a glass from the kitchen, they might ask her to retrieve it. If the floor was dusty, Robina would sometimes now be asked to sweep it. And if she said she was busy, they would get angry.

When she went home to spend time with her own family, Khadija's family demanded that she return sooner than she'd planned.

"You have become arrogant," Khadija cursed. "You are ungrateful."

When Robina turned thirteen, she and her mother agreed that it was better for her not to go there anymore.

❦

ROBINA WAS HOME, back among her family—and the Taliban were gone.

She and her sisters went to the reopened stalls and bought music cassettes. They painstakingly reassembled a collection of Afghan singers, like Ahmad Zahir and Farhad Darya, crooning and drumming about love, ambition, religion, and the future.

When Robina climbed down the mountain to refill their water jugs, she saw new buildings being erected every day. Rubble was cleared away and giant girders rose to the sky. Dirt paths became paved roads, seemingly overnight. Offices were opened for international organizations, like the United Nations and CARE International, which offered food, health care, and educational training, serving the hundreds of thousands of Afghans who stayed in Kabul and the millions of refugees pouring into the city.

Bank buildings, signs for cell phones, streets with crowds

of people, roads filled with cars and bikes, people dodging traffic as they darted across, horns honking, vendors hawking products, the hum of conversations—the cacophony was new, and Robina wasn't sure she liked it.

And there were challenges at home. Her father had always worked sporadically, frequently pocketing the money he earned.

Now he spent long stretches at home, and his behavior became increasingly erratic.

One day, he attacked the house, tearing down the gate and punching through walls, breaking doors.

Robina and her brother confronted him. "Why do you do this?"

"I don't know," he muttered. Then, "I didn't do this."

"But we saw you," Robina said.

"I don't know," he sighed. "No. I haven't done this."

"Was he ever different?" Robina asked her mother shakily that night.

"No," she said. "He was always like this."

"I was ten years old when I was engaged to your father," her mother said as they made dinner. "He was twice my age."

After marrying, they moved to Kabul. Zainab was hired by an American family who came to like and respect her. Thus, when they made plans to return to the States, they invited Zainab's son, Najib, to travel with them and study in America. He wanted to be an engineer.

Omar refused to allow him to go.

"I said to your father, 'But the Americans offered us their

house, pressing the key into my hand.' They also gave me the key to their car. 'Go ahead and stay here,' they told me. 'Everything is yours.'"

Still, Omar refused. Instead, irrationally, in response to her pleas, he demanded that Zainab and the children leave Kabul immediately, to move back to his ancestral village Jalalabad, in southern Afghanistan.

In Jalalabad, they had no land. There were no jobs. They had nothing.

As the family swelled, each child adding to the chaos and pressure, Omar finally admitted the obvious. The move had been a failure. They returned to Kabul. But, of course, the American family was already gone.

"I found work with a new family, the wealthy Afghans I work for now," Zainab continued. "They were kind. They gave us food and fruit to take home, as well as used furniture and our television." Zainab poured her words out to Robina in a torrent, like a rush of muddy water.

When Zainab was wed to Omar, she had been too young to oppose it.

When the foreigners wanted to take Najib to the U.S. for an education, Omar said no.

When they offered their house and car, Omar said no.

When Robina's sister Nadia—just a year older—became a teenager, Omar wed her against her and her mother's wishes.

Now Robina had a request to make. She didn't know what to expect.

"*Madar*," she began. "One day after volleyball practice at *Aschiana*, the American English teacher, Elizabeth, asked me to come to the office. A tall, thin American with a puff of white beard was there. 'I'm Duaine,' he said, and put his hand out to shake mine."

She described how he sat back in a chair and, with Elizabeth translating, asked her what sports she loved.

"Soccer and volleyball," she answered.

"If you love soccer," he said, "then why don't you play on a soccer team?"

"In Afghanistan, girls just play volleyball," Robina said.

"Not anymore."

Soon after, she began playing soccer every week with a new team at a place called the Afghan Center. Then Duaine informed her that she had been selected for a trip to train for soccer in America. If her parents gave permission, she could leave that summer.

Robina looked up at her mother anxiously.

"What about *Padar*?" Robina asked her.

"You are going to America."

the quiet leader

ROBINA, KABUL AND AMERICA

"The seeker is the finder."
—AFGHAN PROVERB

O N JUNE 18, 2004, the morning Robina was to leave for America, she rose at 5 A.M., as usual, for *fajr.*

The night before, she'd packed her bag for the trip—several shirts and pairs of pants, a toothbrush, and pictures of her mother, her father, the family together. She knew the car would be coming early in the morning to take her to the airport.

It would be six weeks before she saw her family again.

"*Madar,* may I sleep next to you?" Robina had asked her mother the night before.

"Yes," Zainab said and smiled, motioning her to lie down beside her on the *toshak.*

They spent the night nestled against each other, and Robina slept well.

When the driver pulled the car up to their house, Ariana and Miriam were already seated inside. Robina hesitated at her doorway. She turned back to her family, all standing in a row to see her off, blinking back tears.

What if the plane crashes? What if I never come back?

Her own eyes began to tear.

"Why don't we come with you to the airport?" Zainab asked gently. It was only twenty minutes by car, and they could take a bus back.

"No," Robina said. "Don't come. If you come with me to the airport, I'll feel more sad."

Robina felt as if she were rooted into the ground.

Salma gave her a hug and whispered, "I could come. I don't mind."

"No," Robina said, trying to smile. "It is better to say good-bye at home, than to know you are going home without me."

She pulled herself away from her family and climbed into the car. Ariana and Miriam greeted her. She had already practiced with them at the Afghan Center. Their faces were also streaked with tears. She peered through the window at her family still gathered before the house.

What will happen to me?

The car drove off. And stopped to pick up Samira, weeping uncontrollably as she entered the car. The girls rushed to comfort her.

"We're all in this together."

"Don't worry. We will be safe together in America."

"You will not be alone."

⟨❧⟩

DURING THE THREE-HOUR flight from Kabul to Dubai, Robina brooded, worrying about what lay ahead.

What if the plane crashes?

What if I don't really know how to kick or shoot the ball—what if I am humiliated?

At Dubai, Barbara Goodno ushered them onto the Emirates plane to America. The clouds were like landscapes, the plane plunging through the white drifts as if they were banks of snow, the world brilliantly white.

I'm inside the clouds!

When they arrived at JFK, they boarded a connecting flight to Reagan National Airport in Washington, D.C. There, they staggered into Barbara's car, for the drive to her and Duaine's house.

Their home was made of red brick and tucked away from the road, among willows, oaks, and gardens.

"Welcome," Barbara said, leading them upstairs and separating them into two, large neat rooms, each with a king-sized bed. They dropped their bags and fell asleep next to one another almost immediately.

Robina shared a room with Ariana, Samira, and Miriam. She was still getting to know her new teammates, and the process had been troubling.

When Duaine had first brought them together at the

Afghan Center, the other girls were not friendly. They mocked Robina's mother's daily work as a maid and the dark shade of Robina's skin.

The two sisters, Freshta and Laila, who spoke English, were already close with Duaine.

"Nobody is taking *you* to America," Freshta once told Robina, before they left. "We will talk with Duaine and get you kicked out."

"Okay," Robina shot back. "Go ahead."

The first morning in America, Robina was the first one up. She did her *fajr* prayer and then padded downstairs. Barbara was already in the kitchen.

"Good morning," Barbara said, in a cheerful voice.

Robina understood the spirit, if not the words, and smiled. She studied Barbara as she moved easily through the kitchen, heating up milk in the microwave, pulling out plates from the shelves. After a few days, Robina was ready to try herself.

Waking early as usual, she went downstairs. She poured milk into a large Pyrex measuring cup and punched buttons on the microwave. She set out plates, placing a slice of bread on each of them. Her teammates entered the kitchen and broke into surprised smiles. Robina smiled back.

After breakfast, they ran to the pool dressed modestly in long shorts and T-shirts. The first day, almost none of them knew how to swim, so they clung to the tiled sides, or dipped their hands and toes into the cold depths, ripples circling across the surface.

The next week, Roya gave them swimming lessons. The other girls splashed through the shallow end of the pool. Robina found that she loved to dive.

She'd climb onto the small diving board and dive into the deepest end of the pool, plummeting down into the clear, aqua water. Then, in a burst, she'd propel herself upward, rising to take a breath of air.

That first week in D.C., they also practiced soccer. The team was scheduled to compete in the Afghan Sports Federation's annual Fourth of July Afghan-American Soccer Cup in Virginia.

Sunday morning, July 4, Robina and her teammates piled into the car and headed to the field near Barbara and Duaine's house for one last practice. Ali ran them through some basic drills—passing the ball back and forth, taking shots on net.

One drill was particularly difficult. Starting at the edge of the field, a ball at their feet, their challenge was to cross the terrain to the goal at the other side, dribbling at the fastest possible pace without losing control. It was a balance they constantly miscalculated, the ball skidding away out of reach when they went too fast, stumbling over themselves and falling hopelessly behind when they went too slow. It was difficult to reach the end of the field without everything falling apart. When that morning's practice ended, the girls climbed back into the car. It had rained overnight and the sky was still overcast, a noncommittal gray.

When they pulled up to the Soccer Cup site in Springfield,

two or three grassy fields were marked off in a larger clearing, with hundreds of people milling around. Robina got out and stretched. An older Afghan woman noticed her and greeted her with a "*Salaam.*"

"*Salaam, Khala jan,*" Hello dear aunt, Robina answered.

The crowd gathered on the grass. Robina heard snatches of Dari and Pashto.

The game began, played against a select team of Afghan-Americans. Ali stayed on the sidelines, talking the girls through the game. He shooed them into position, alerted them to opportunities to pass, to push through holes in the defense, to score.

Robina felt terrified, certain she would blunder on the field, be humiliated and exposed before the crowd.

That fear stayed with her throughout the game. But on the field, she appeared perfectly poised and she battled fiercely for every ball.

The game ended in a tie, 0–0.

She and her team had faced Afghans in America and found themselves equal to the task—even though they'd missed passes, lost opportunities, and hadn't scored a goal.

But their team had played hard, with honor, and *they had not lost.*

After the game, the girls lined up to shake hands with the other team. Then both teams ran around the perimeter of the field, as the spectators applauded and cheered.

The girls joined the crowd, settling along the grass to watch the men's championship game. They chattered in Dari and Pashto, greeting people who came by, some with tears in their eyes, to ask questions about life back in Afghanistan.

There was an awards ceremony after the men's championship game ended. Both girls' soccer teams were called up to the podium, where they were given medals.

Robina's first soccer medal.

Wait till I show Madar.

⚜

IT WAS A blistering day in August when Robina arrived back in Kabul. The car dropped her off at her front door, which was unlocked. She walked into the main room, where her younger siblings were playing on the floor. At the sight of her, they leapt to their feet and threw their arms around her.

"Did you win the championship? Tell us!"

"Well, this was my first time going to America," she said carefully. "So even though we didn't win, it's okay, because it was our first time."

Her parents and older brother Najib were at work, and didn't have cell phones. So Robina napped until her brother shook her awake.

"Robina *jan,* get up!" he cried. "*Madar* is home."

Zainab walked through the door. She and Robina embraced.

"I am happy you are home safe," Zainab whispered.

Soon, Najib came in, and Robina told him about the tournaments and her adventures.

"Keep it up," he urged. "Keep learning."

NOW, BACK IN Kabul, Robina loves to practice with the girls, who have become close friends. She yearns to compete for Afghanistan, but for now, she is happy teaching the soccer skills she has learned to other girls, who also want to play but haven't yet had the chance. When her schoolmates find out she has been to America to play soccer, they beg her to teach them.

Robina is determined to start a team, as soon as she can find a suitable field. She begins with teaching her sister Salma in their backyard, calling out stern instructions and correcting her form. Soon her sister joins her at the Friday practices.

In America, girls rode bicycles down the street, drove cars, played soccer on grass fields. Robina wants girls in Afghanistan to be able to do the same.

But she is constantly reminded of the road still ahead.

Her friend Tamana no longer plays volleyball and her family has removed her from school. Sometimes Zainab, who works near their house, will bring back a letter Tamana's written for Robina.

You're very lucky, she writes to Robina one day.

ROBINA'S FAMILY HAS moved across Kabul. When Robina went to America, her family lived in a house in Chelsatoon, with two rooms—a kitchen and a living room. There was also a small place for the bathroom, where they could wash privately.

But shortly after she returned, the owners raised the rent beyond what the family could afford.

Their new house, built by Robina's uncle, has only one room. It is located high in the hills.

When her new neighbors find out Robina has been to America—a mistake that she let it slip—the teasing begins.

"Oh, you have relations with Americans," boys call at her as she carries water up the mountain to their house every morning. "Does that mean you're American?"

They gather around her, hurling statements that make her cheeks burn.

She comes home crying, and her mother goes with her the next day. When the small boys gather at the edges of the steep, rocky path, Zainab whirls on them, roaring through the grill of her *burqa*, "I am not a visitor here! This is my house. You will not say such things."

She moves toward them bathed in light blue robes; they scatter without a word.

"Afghan people are very conservative," Zainab explains to Robina later that night. "From the time of Daud Khan, Afghans have been consumed by the bitterness of the world. You should have been done with school by now, but during the Taliban's time, the conservatives didn't allow you. Now they are gone. But change takes time."

One Friday morning, Robina sits on the bus to practice, reading a sports magazine.

"What is that?" asks the girl next to her, curious. "Where are you going?"

"I'm going to play soccer."

"Your family allows you to play soccer?"

"Yes," Robina says. She studies the girl. "Are you interested?"

"My brother doesn't even allow me to go to school," the girl says softly. "Playing soccer is out of the question."

between two worlds

I GREW UP in two worlds—a private, Afghan world at home, a public, American one outside.

My elementary school was across town, so my sister, brother, and I met a yellow school bus every morning, its stop about three blocks from our Connecticut house.

I loved school. From Bucks Hill Elementary to North End Middle School to Wilby High, I always felt good in the classroom. I *liked* to study, actually.

Until high school, however, I usually went home after classes. There, as I first remember them, were the language, the foods, and the culture of Afghanistan.

In the years my siblings and I were in grammar and middle school, both my parents worked for the same company, Winchester Electronics: my father, Mohammad, as an engineer, and my mother, Bibi, on the assembly line, second shift.

Because of her hours, I didn't get to see my mother during the week, only on weekends.

Then, my sister, Zohra, and I would sit on the high kitchen stools, chatting to our mom about our week. We spoke in Pashto as she whipped up aromatic *aush,* a yogurt-based noodle soup with beans and ground beef, and *qaboli palaw,* a rice dish mixed with fragrant almonds, raisins, and cardamom. Or *mantu,* steamed dumplings stuffed with sautéed onions and minced beef, and *bolani,* flattened fried dough filled with potatoes and leeks.

To this day, I will go a long way to taste these foods homemade.

Other kids enjoyed after-school programs, joined the local youth soccer team, or acted in school plays. On weekends, my sister and I were learning *khamak dozi,* the Afghan embroidery endemic to Kandahar, where my mother was born and raised.

She was adamant that we learn this from her. It wasn't so much that it was Afghan, but that it was an art—and believe me, it wasn't easy to learn.

She started us when we were young. I was only five, so naturally I protested. I would poke my finger with the needle, hoping she'd take pity on me.

I wanted to be outside. I'd stare longingly out the window at friends from the neighborhood gathered in the playground across the street from our house, playing kickball or pushing one another on swings. I wanted to be out running, jumping, competing with them, not sitting on the couch with a needle and cloth.

"*Mor,* may I go outside and play?" I'd implore her.

But my mother was determined. "You need to learn this first, Awista *jan*. It is part of our heritage."

꧁✿꧂

AS WE GREW up, we were taught how to read the Qur'an in Arabic, the language of Islam's holy book, and how to recite its *surahs* as we prayed.

And our parents told us stories.

The Afghanistan my mother and father conjured for us was a simple and carefree one, a nation of wide spaces and skies of lapis brilliance. It was a land of gorgeous mosques, tiled with intricate design and colors, even in the most remote of places.

On the weekends, my father would make us an Afghan breakfast of sautéed onions and tomatoes with eggs; Afghan flat bread; and milk *chay* infused with cardamom, my favorite. Sitting at our round breakfast table, chin resting on my hands, I savored the tales about him and his brothers climbing and tumbling out of trees; or racing through the beautiful gardens of Arghandab, a place popular for family outings; or getting up in the dark before sunrise each Friday to go to the *masjid* to pray; or how he and his friends would pull pranks on their neighbors on Alokozai Street, where they lived in Kandahar.

"What kind of pranks, *Baba*?"

"Oh, little things, like we would switch fruits from one basket to another in the market," he'd say with a glint in his eye. "The older women would get confused and we would run away laughing."

I knew that without the wars I too might have spent my childhood running through the gardens, snatching fresh fruit or scrambling up my family's own trees. I daydreamed about Afghanistan, imagined lying on the flat roof of our house, breathing in the fresh evening air, counting the stars my parents insisted shone brighter there than anywhere else.

WHEN THE SOVIETS occupied Afghanistan in 1979, my family had gone into exile. Though my father and mother had built a prosperous life for us in the United States, they ached to return home. Yet with each passing year it seemed more unlikely.

Like so many children of exile, I wanted to see my motherland. But one war evolved into another, each more devastating than the last, so that I too began to lose hope.

I was in fourth grade when the Soviet forces left Afghanistan in 1989. The country, used as a battleground between the two superpowers for ten years, was suddenly forgotten. Without a plan for reconstruction, with a third of its citizens refugees, with much of the various tribes armed and supported financially by the West and their allies, factions sprung up, and civil war savaged the land.

Homes, buildings, whole villages were destroyed, along with the prospect of many Afghans returning home.

Then, in 1996, a group of young students of Islam spoke out against the devastation that continuous war had inflicted on Afghanistan, including the corruption of Islamic values. They began to form a small, fervent army determined to seize back the country.

These students, or *Taliban,* promised to re-instill religious purity and establish peace.

Peace. The younger generations of Afghans had no memory of a time without war and destruction. The Taliban's promise was enticing.

At first, arms and funds from Western countries bolstered the Taliban. Then their regime took hold. Before people could catch their breath, new laws were put in place: Men were forbidden to shave their beards. Music was banned. Dancing at weddings was outlawed. Women could not leave their home without a close male relative, and schools for girls were shut down.

The laws became extensive, determining almost every aspect of life. Male and female violators were punished in brutal, public demonstrations that sometimes included amputations and executions.

The Taliban's reinterpretation of Shari'a Law—laws based on the Qur'an—left many wondering: Would Afghanistan ever be free of tragedy?

Over time, conversations at our dinner table changed from colorful stories of my parents' past to intense political discussions. I could hear the frustration and sadness in my father's voice as his dream of returning home eroded, worn away by each successive year of carnage and desolation.

"Afghanistan is no longer the country I remember," he lamented.

As the nation spiraled further away from its own identity, my mother struggled to keep some of its traditions alive. She was glad she had taught us sewing and embroidery.

"I loved it," she'd reminisce with a dreamy smile. "I made my own clothes growing up, even my wedding dress."

All through our home were the throws, pillows, curtains, and tablecloths she'd embroidered with her own designs. And soon my embroidered designs, some of which won awards, would adorn our kitchen table also.

There is a photo of my mother and her four sisters when they were young women in Kabul during the 1970s. They are lounging near a pool, their slight figures in bell-bottoms, their long, black hair shining down their backs. I'd stare at the photo and then watch the daily newscasts, where film clips of women shrouded in *burqa* blue were replayed over and over again.

It was hard to reconcile that version of the country with my parents' memories.

IN OCTOBER 2001, the United States, along with coalition forces, entered Afghanistan to remove the Taliban from power. The leadership quickly retreated.

This began an influx of millions of Afghan refugees returning to their homeland. Many walked or came by horse-drawn carts from neighboring Pakistan and Iran; others flew in from around the world.

The door to Afghanistan was open.

sisters

FRESHTA AND LAILA, FROM PAKISTAN TO KABUL

"I jumped inside the ring, all of me. Dance, then, and I danced."

—NAOMI SHIHAB NYE

RESHTA AND LAILA entered Afghanistan for the first time in the back of a truck, perched atop their family's carpets, mats, clothes, and pillows. They were eleven and twelve. Along with their mother, cousin, and siblings, they rattled through the Khyber Pass on the twenty-four-hour journey from their home in Peshawar, Pakistan. It was the summer of 2002.

The previous October, American planes had launched a bombing strike within Afghanistan, to drive out the Taliban.

Then it happened. Kabul was reclaimed. Hafiz, the girls' father, left immediately, taking a truck across the border to secure housing for the family's return. Through an uncle traveling from Kabul to Pakistan, he sent a message. He'd found a two-story house, right in the heart of Kabul.

They left within days.

"Why is this truck going so slowly?" Laila complained.

"Did you see the street?" Arzo, her mother, answered quietly.

Laila looked down and gasped—the road had been bombed to rubble. There was no road.

"You're between Pakistan and Afghanistan," her mother continued. "War happened here."

"I thought it was going to be beautiful," Laila murmured, unable to erase her accusing tone.

"It was," Arzo said.

Laila stared at the crumbling buildings, the smashed streets, the empty storefronts, the stretches of flat, bombed-out land.

In Pakistan, their home—a small, comfortable mud house of five rooms that their father built—had been nestled in a neighborhood of Afghan refugees and expatriates. Their home was surrounded by multistoried glass-paneled mansions, with swimming pools the children splashed in daily.

Freshta and her sisters swam in the nearby river.

Some of the families had cars to take them shopping every day. Freshta and Laila walked to the one-room, windowless general store just a few blocks from where they lived. The store sold beans, potatoes, buttons, needles, cookies, and candy, with toys piled on a bed outside.

Some men drove to work in the mornings; their father, Hafiz, rode a bicycle to the train station.

Freshta and Laila loved their home. Hafiz had bought the land for their house, and over the years of exile the girls' parents had nurtured a large, fragrant garden enclosed by high stone walls. A peach tree flowered in one corner, growing alongside grape vines, pomegranates, okra, corn, cauliflower, eggplant, and peppers. They hung a swing between the trees. All ten children would take turns on it in the warm afternoons.

In the heat of the summer, the family pulled all their beds out into the yard. As evening fell, they would drift outside, drinking sweet-smelling cups of *chay*, chatting quietly, to sleep finally under the stars.

Sometimes the four sisters would stare at the sky, trying to spot which star was the brightest. Fresh breezes whisked away the heavy heat, rustling their hair and the light sheets over their bodies. Whispering and laughing, they'd stay awake until sleep overtook them.

Arzo and Hafiz had escaped from Afghanistan in 1980, vowing to come back when the war was over. Twenty years later, they were raising ten children in Pakistan, still waiting.

Arzo built a picture of Afghanistan in her children's minds through the stories she told them. She described thick carpets covering the floors of the schools, how her shoes would sink into the soft, colored rugs. In her telling, all the rooms were clean, bright, the walls scrubbed so perfectly that they reflected blinding shards of sunlight.

"And when you walk outside the buildings," she'd tell them, "the ground is blanketed in flowers."

Freshta and Laila loved to watch cricket, a popular sport in Pakistan. Arzo told them that, in Kabul, basketball and volleyball courts teemed with girls, exercising in unison, lunging for the ball as they scrimmaged under the coach's screeching whistles. She spoke so persuasively that Freshta and Laila could see the volleyball team spiking balls over the net, drilling serves, balls arching endlessly over the taut white net, like the spray of a fountain.

In Pakistan, they wore Punjabi clothes, long colorful shirts with a slit down the side, worn over loose pants, and no head scarves. They followed the news about Afghanistan: the women wearing the *burqas,* bodies fully covered, faces hidden behind mesh.

"When I was growing up, women wore skirts—anything they wanted," she said. "Women had rights. Even what to wear and what not to wear."

Freshta complained that she did not understand the edicts.

"Why can't they have the same rights now?" Laila chimed in.

"It's the Taliban," Arzo said, turning away from the television.

"Were there really executions, *Madar*?" Freshta whispered.

"Yes, there were."

One December day, Laila was watching TV and saw Kabul covered in white.

"What is that?" she asked, astonished.

"It's snow," Arzo told her, with a smile. But then it faded. "Some people will die this winter because of the cold."

That summer rain stopped and rivers evaporated. The TV showed carcasses of cattle, horses, even sheep. A terrible drought had begun.

Arzo's face was pained. "Soon it will be people." She turned away. "It's hard living in war."

Arzo distracted her children by describing a movie theater in Kabul, which, she said, was larger than every other building, its screen stretching as high as their house.

She spun stories about the massive peaks encircling the city, rising into the sky, an earthen fortress protecting the people of Kabul.

"I want to go," Freshta would say over and over, as they ate dinner, sat outside, wove carpets.

"Right now it's very bad. We can't go there because it's very dangerous."

"When *can* we go, then?"

"I don't know," Arzo admitted. "When the war is over."

THE GIRLS' UNCLES, Omid and Qasim, arrived as refugees from Afghanistan and took up residence in their household.

Freshta and Laila, along with Meena and Jamila, their other sisters, and their oldest brother, Khalid, were drafted into learning from their uncles the craft of carpet weaving.

Khalid was put in charge of managing the daily weaving. He'd go to the rug store in town and bring home the map for a carpet (the pattern and coloring sketched out) along with bundles of hand-dyed wool and the string, needles, and knives needed for weaving.

To start a carpet, each of the five siblings took a position in a line along the bottom of the loom. With the map of the design hung before them, Laila and Khalid worked first, stitching the outline of the designs in black thread, defining petals and stems of flowers. Once the shapes were sketched across the loom, Jamila, Meena, and Freshta began to weave in the colors with small stubs of bright wool.

Khalid plugged in his tape recorder and played his collection of Indian songs, and they belted out the lyrics together.

The music's rhythm helped the weavers keep pace. Laila also listened to the music their weaving made. The five of them worked together, each producing a different sound: the rip of the wool, the jab of the needle, the click of the knotted threads pulled tight.

Bawar nakardaneest, Laila thought. We're good.

Sometimes, though, they'd puncture their hands, which would bleed.

And the wool's animal smell! Hair came off on their hands. The five of them tied scarves around their noses and mouths. The stench was like fruit left out too long to rot. When they cut the fabric, dust came off in clouds, causing them to cough and choke.

"That's not good," Arzo said frequently, worried. "Let's gather the wool and hang it outside."

They lifted the huge skeins of wool, hung them on a line in the yard, and beat them with brooms until the covering of dust was gone.

Laila liked to work with very sharp knives, and she worked quickly. One afternoon, the thread snapped and the knife jerked up, slashing her eyelid, blood leaking down her face. But still, she finished her rows.

At the end of each day's weaving, hunched over the loom, moving forward inch by meticulous inch, their entire bodies ached. All five stumbled into bed, into dead sleep.

Still, they took pride in the beauty of the emerging design. They exclaimed when the carpet was finally flipped over and the tufts of knotted threads were transformed into glorious flowers, snaking vines, and intricate patterns.

One day, the fan in the workroom was broken. Arzo fiddled with the generator.

"Did you turn the power off?" she asked Laila.

Laila couldn't remember, so she flipped the switch. But this turned the power on, sending roughly two hundred volts of current coursing through the line.

Arzo had already opened the generator, her hand on the fuse. She screamed.

Khalid burst into the room as his mother collapsed on the floor. Thinking she'd fainted, he grabbed the bucket of water nearby and splashed water on her. Arzo's body convulsed, her skin blackening.

At the sight, Laila screamed, running out of the room. Qasim charged in. He grabbed Arzo's hand away from the fuse. Her skin was burned, peeling from her fingers, exposing bone.

He lifted her onto his back and ran outside, shouting, "We need a car! We must go to the hospital!"

. . .

She couldn't leave her bed for two months. A doctor came daily to cut away the dead skin sticking her fingers together.

It would be a long time before Arzo was healed.

Months later, they were on the road to Kabul.

〜✲〜

THE TRUCK FINALLY shuddered to a stop before a building, half-built, half-ruin. Their father emerged from it, waving. The gray mud façade had been stripped away in broad gashes, exposing the guts of the walls, the haphazardly stacked bricks.

A large window on the second floor was smothered in plastic sheeting, with a few wooden boards tacked across it. A balcony, possibly grand once, hung lopsidedly, stained and rotting. Bullet holes riddled the walls. There were no doors.

As in Pakistan, a river ran beside their house. But it had shrunk into a shallow puddle, leaving steep, dry sides. Barren trees lined the dusty banks, branches slumping into the water and lying on the stagnant surface.

After helping Arzo and all the children out of the truck, Hafiz turned to the driver.

"Can you help me clear some bricks?" he asked, offering a few afghanis.

Together they entered the house and emerged again, hauling bags of bricks, which had fallen from the walls and the ceiling.

Laila stepped through the black open square of their front door.

Over the next few months, she got used to the peeling walls and learned which ceiling spots leaked. She became skilled at climbing the metal ladder up to the second floor.

One morning, Arzo tripped and crashed down those steps, injuring her back, knees, and neck.

Several days later, one-year-old Amir crawled across the floor toward a hole. Arzo saw him and grasped his foot just before he plunged down.

Their first winter, snow came through the ceiling and the windows. Laila caught the flakes in her hand as they floated down through the house.

As time went on, they draped laundry over the precarious balcony and on lines in the yard. They added red curtains to the windows, even those without glass.

Over the faded, patterned carpet from Pakistan, red rugs were laid, and crushed red velvet pillows were piled in the corner.

Hafiz, a welder, built furniture for his family—a small TV stand, large iron boxes for their clothes. He whitewashed all the walls.

Another family lived on the ground floor. Strangers.

They heard their fights through the thin floor, echoing up the metal staircase. The patriarch downstairs was frail and afraid of his oldest son, who beat his sister if she wore jeans or showed too much of her hair.

One day, through a hole in their floor, Laila saw the son slam his fist into his sister's head, as she bit her hand in order not to scream.

"*Madar*," Laila cried. "Something is happening downstairs."

Her mother climbed quickly and firmly down the stairs and confronted the young man.

"If you want something, why don't you say it in a friendly way?" she said quietly. He stalked away.

Finally, it got to be too much. During another beating, Hafiz clattered down the steps, charged the brother, and flung him against the wall.

"You are not the only man around here with fists," he said. "If you touch her again, we will hurt you."

The family, especially Freshta and Laila, were shaken by the violence of their neighbors; they were also unsettled by the war-stained city. *It's made everything, and everyone, strange,* Laila thought.

It was a mistake to come here, Freshta said to herself.

They had had friends in Pakistan. They had had a nice house to themselves. Neighbors were friendly. Their family was happy.

"I want to go back to Pakistan," Freshta finally admitted to Arzo.

"I would rather live in my own country," Arzo said. "It is your country, too."

ONE DAY LAILA walked to the bazaar in new blue jeans her mother had bought her.

Boys jeered.

"You are very cute!" one called out. "Nice jeans."

Laila turned on them. "My parents bought these for me. Who are you to tell me what to wear and what not to wear?"

"Look at this!" A boy pointed, amused at her challenge.

"What is she saying to us?" another boy shouted.

"If you keep talking, I'll call the police," said Laila.

She forced herself to keep walking, to buy the glittery bracelets she had come for. But she couldn't stop herself from running home once the purchases were clutched in her hand.

She told her mother, in tears.

"You told me that women here are dressing like this, that they can wear skirts above their knees."

"Before, that was okay, but now it's changed."

"But I thought the war was over!"

"You can't do everything at once," Laila's mother told her softly. "It has to go step by step."

Arzo retrieved a box of old photographs. She pulled out a picture of herself as a girl, about the same age as Laila. She and her aunt were outside in a park, wearing skirts above their knees and T-shirts.

"That looks nice," Laila said, bitterly.

"Yes, the culture has changed since I was your age," Arzo said.

Freshta and Laila were enrolled in the first grade at the Nawan-i-Guzargha School, just a short walk from their house.

Both were attending school for the first time. They donned the uniform of black pants and long button-down black coat, with a white scarf tucked around the head.

In almost every way, school diverged from their mother's stories. There were students of all ages, some entering school for the first time at fifteen years old. With the influx of refugees, classes were set up in three or four three-hour sessions a day, for both boys and girls, although in separate classes.

There was no running water or toilet paper; there were no tissues or heaters. Once, a bomb was nearly smuggled into the school when a student was approached by a stranger and asked to release a "bird" inside the principal's office. She refused and reported it. The school was locked down. From then on, no one was allowed to bring in even the smallest packages, even fruit picked that morning from their own farms and orchards. Every bag was searched.

Laila embraced school. She stuck to her promise to learn what she had to do to become a doctor, to search for a way to help her mother. At home, while Freshta lounged on the *toshaks,* Laila sat in a corner studying for hours.

The sisters were in the same grade. Laila earned top grades in her classroom and Freshta took second place. After achieving the top position, Laila was eligible to become a teacher's assistant, but she refused, preferring to simply study with friends. She deferred the position to her sister.

Freshta leapt at the assignment. She loved giving orders, standing in front of the class, leading a session. She didn't hesitate to use the ruler to whack disorderly students if they caused disruptions during her lessons.

AFTER SCHOOL, FRESHTA and Laila would do errands for their mother if Arzo was having one of her "bad days." Both girls noticed when their mother paused on the precarious landing of the stairs, hesitated before lifting a pot, or stood still for a moment in the center of a room. They understood that she was fragile, like a vase whose smooth surface would crack at the lightest tap.

One afternoon, Arzo asked them, "Would you bring these rounds of dough to the bakery down the road?" The moist dough would be baked in the bakery's large clay oven. And, while the two of them were out, "Would you please fill the larger water jug from the well?"

The girls left their house. Although it was the first week of October, the fall winds had yet to descend on the city and sweep it into a new season. Summer still covered Kabul like a lid, heavy and hot, baking the bowl of the city.

Like the thousands of new refugees who arrived every day, the sisters had been living in the city for only a short while. It was hard to adjust to the sporadic electricity, the open sewer ditches along the roads, the smell, intensified by the heat, and the barren land and bombed-out buildings.

More than three million refugees had returned to Afghanistan from Pakistan, Iran, and other countries, the vast majority settling in Kabul. A city that had had a prewar population of 400,000 was cracking under the influx of millions.

The additional people strained the power systems, overran the sewers, and battered down already broken roads. Yet when the girls went outside, the streets were quiet. *Where do people go?* Laila wondered.

It was different, though, at the water well and pump—a central gathering place for all the children living nearby.

It took both sisters to lift the large jug once it was filled with water and to stagger home, each clutching a handle.

That day, as they lugged the jug home, they heard a commotion down the street. A tall, light-skinned older man in a *paran tumban,* the traditional flowing pants and a long, loose shirt, was handing out candy to a growing crowd of children.

He noticed the two sisters and waved. Freshta and Laila set down the water jug and approached him curiously. He looked tired, but smiled as he gave out the candy. It was obvious that he did not speak Dari.

Freshta took a few pieces of the candy and fixed him with her appraising stare as she put them into her mouth. *Good.* She motioned to him, gesturing up the hill, toward their house. She mimed drinking tea.

He'd received offers before, from virtually every Afghan he'd met since first entering the country several weeks ago— part of the country's famed hospitality to guests. Not wanting to impose, he'd turned every one down.

Now, to his own surprise, he agreed.

"Duaine Goodno," he said, and extended his hand.

⟨❧⟩

HAFIZ GREETED THEM at the house, and they climbed up a thin metal staircase without a railing. Duaine followed cautiously; his eyesight had been damaged from a recent stroke.

Their first attempts at communication were halting and awkward.

"How—old—are—you?" Duaine mouthed at Laila.

She looked amused.

"*Nam-e shoma che-st?*" she asked.

Using hands and fingers and expressions, they slowly built a series of understandings. He pointed at himself and said, "Duaine!"

The sisters look at each other. Freshta did the same: "Freshta!" She told Laila to try it too. "Laila," she said, pointing to herself.

Duaine continued to visit, and taught the two girls a bit more English. He was welcomed by the entire family, particularly Hafiz. Soon though, rumors began to circulate in the crowded community. Questions came sharp and furious from neighbors—accusations that he had come to convert the community to Christianity.

"I will handle it," Hafiz told Duaine.

But in response, Duaine began varying his route.

Sometimes, when he arrived at the house, Freshta and Laila ran outside and frantically waved him away if the neighbors were home. Even so, his relationship with the family deepened.

With Arzo and Hafiz's blessing, he hired the girls' cousin Zarina to teach Laila and Freshta English. She also became a translator for him and the family.

Through the cousin, he asked Arzo and Hafiz if they would allow Laila and Freshta to change schools. He had contacts at Kabul International Academy, a new school with a rigorous English curriculum. He took the girls on a visit. The school was clean and neat, with twelve students per class, including boys and girls, each with a single desk. Outside the building was a sports complex, with a grass soccer field and a volleyball court. Girls could play.

"Do you want to go here?" Duaine asked the girls.

"Yes!" Laila said.

As classes started, Laila learned her first complete English sentence; mimicking her teacher: "Don't do that."

⁕

IN FEBRUARY 2004, Duaine heard about a new program, the Afghan Youth Sports Exchange, proposing to teach leadership to young Afghan girls through sports.

"I have two girls who might be interested," he e-mailed the organizer.

gathering of the girls

FRESHTA AND LAILA, KABUL, DECEMBER 2005

> *"The connection to the Friend*
> *Is secret and very fragile."*
> —RUMI

ADAR, MAY I invite the girls from our soccer team to spend the night tomorrow?" Laila asks. It's a Friday night, in December 2005, and she and Freshta have just returned from soccer practice.

The Roots of Peace field is a ten-minute walk from their house. Their fingers are still stiff from the cold, their faces flushed from the hours they've spent pelting a soccer ball across the hard, frozen ground.

Arzo is putting rice to boil on the *goz*, a small gas stove. Laila joins her in the small cooking area—there is just room for two people—and warms her hands at the flame.

Arzo continues preparing dinner with her slow, sure movements.

"There's a tournament!" Freshta yells out from the square main room, where she is slouched on a *toshak,* watching television. "We have to go to Hindu Kush Field tomorrow."

Arzo sits cross-legged on a *destarkhan,* a cloth spread over the floor, and begins chopping spinach on a board.

"After practice today, Halima approached us," Laila tells her mother, referring to their assistant coach. "She told us we are playing well."

It is true, despite the fact that over the past few weeks, the team has been whittled down. Ariana has been too busy with work, she said, to practice with them, and the two youngest players, Nadia and Deena, have abruptly disappeared.

The five remaining players have practiced regularly for more than a year since their return to Kabul last August. Now, as December begins, their individual games have fitted together, like puzzle pieces pressed into place. Slender Laila and Miriam on defense, sturdy Robina and Freshta on offense, and wiry Samira waiting in the net.

They have clicked into a team. At practice, passes sail across the field, landing at the feet of a teammate, already there, ready for the kick. On the field, they communicate with secret winks, nods, and hand gestures. They hold a practice scrimmage against the employees of Roots of Peace—older, larger security guards; their one-legged coach, Fawad; and Halima—and win.

. . .

After their practice earlier in the day, as they were picking up their bags, and replacing their head scarves, Halima had walked over.

"Have you heard about the tournament?" she asked.

They shook their heads.

"It is being organized by the Olympic Committee, which is looking to start our first women's national team. More than a dozen teams have registered to compete in a tournament." Halima smiled. "I think you girls could do well," she told them. "Try to register tomorrow."

Laila looks to her mother.

"The tournament has already started, *Madar,* but Halima is hopeful that we will still be able to enter as our own team. Then Miriam, Robina, and Samira can come back with us."

Arzo listens as she scrapes the spinach into a pot. "Since there is no school, I give you permission," she says. Schools shut down for weeks in the winter, because there is not enough city power to heat the classrooms.

"In fact," she continues, "why not invite your teammates over tonight? Without school to worry about, you can have fun, and all go together to register."

Laila hugs her mother.

That night, Miriam, Robina, and Samira arrive. After dinner, Hafiz suggests that the five girls take one of the larger rooms for the night, rather than cram into Freshta and Laila's tiny bedroom.

"Why don't you use my room?" says Nathalie, their sister-in-law. She lives with their brother Asif in the largest bedroom. "Asif *jan* and I will stay in your room tonight."

Laila smiles. "Thank you, *Khwar jan.*"

She and Freshta direct the three girls into the large, yellow room. The girls pile their bags in the corner, ignoring the sound of the gushing water pipe in the bathroom next door and the sheen of water along the wall, glowing like tears. A plastic sheet covers the room's only window. A nearby bomb blast shattered the glass, and replacing it is expensive.

"I know what we can do!" Freshta says, jumping up. She leads them back out to the table in the main room. They pull over a bench and chairs and sit. Freshta opens her laptop and clicks through photos taken from their trip to America.

"Remember how we acted?" Miriam laughs. "We were so bad. We complained about *everything.*"

"No salt allowed at Barbara's."

"Limp sandwiches in Cleveland."

"Small dorm rooms in Connecticut!"

"Why did we do that?" Laila laughs. "We were such complainers."

As each photo appears on the screen, the girls interrupt one another, retelling stories of whatever they remember, giggling at their most embarrassing moments.

"Samira *jan,* remember when you hid under a tree and we searched for hours?"

Samira blushes. It started when they visited the Embassy of Afghanistan in D.C. during the first week of their trip. Samira asked to use their phone to call her family. The ambassador's handsome young son helped her. Afterward, the other girls circled around, eyebrows suggestively raised, inquiring about Samira's new "friendship." They continued their teasing in Connecticut. One day at practice, it was too much: Samira ran off, plunging into the woods on the school campus and settling at the base of a tree. She fell asleep. A few hours later she walked back to the main student building. As she entered the clatter of the school cafeteria, her teammates greeted her with shouts: "We were frantic! We thought you were lost! We looked everywhere for you!"

"Miriam *jan,* remember the dog? He just wanted to play with you, but your screams! I've never heard anyone scream like that before," says Robina.

Miriam laughs. While in Connecticut, she left practice to use the restroom. Coming back, she tumbled down the steep hill above the grassy practice field. Lifting herself, she was met by a heaving, jowly dog, its soft wet nose rubbing against her own. *"Madar!"* she shrieked, twisting away and burying her head in her hands, crying.

They continue through the pictures, pausing for shots of the Ayub family, their comfortable home, photos of each of the girls lounging on their soft, cushioned couches; they'd even taken photos of the spiced beans and rice on the kitchen table. Before Laila traveled to America, she'd been told Afghan-Americans had "lost the culture." But *Khala jan,* Aunt, had prepared any dish they asked for: *raut,* a sweet, dense bread-cake spiced with cardamom; on other nights *mantu, bolani, palaw.*

Like home.

After Freshta returned from her American trip, friends commented on the lower necklines among the Afghan-Americans in her photos. But Freshta told them, "If you don't wear a scarf, or your neckline is a little low, it doesn't mean that you're not a Muslim. They are Muslims from the heart."

· · ·

Night falls and the house grows dark and cold. The girls tug two or three blankets over them. They light the *bokhari,* a heater in the shape of a barrel, with a small round opening at the top for kindling.

They've arranged their mats in a row, over the carpet.

Laila and Miriam find places next to each other.

When they were in America, Miriam confided in Laila about the loss of her father. Laila cried with her. Afterward, Laila vowed privately to help Miriam any way she could.

Soccer was one way. When Miriam's shots went askew, Laila offered gentle advice.

"Some people would laugh at me for that mistake," Miriam would say.

"I won't, Miriam *jan,*" Laila replied. "Never."

As the two try to fall asleep, they pull a shared blanket over their bodies. Beneath it, they whisper together well past midnight, remembering, wondering about their future, and about the tournament tomorrow.

❧

AFTER SIGNING UP for the tournament on Saturday morning, the team arrives at Hindu Kush Field that afternoon. Freshta is astounded. Girls are everywhere—thirty, forty, fifty of them.

Girls—tall, thin, thick, short—all practicing, balancing balls on their knees, passing the ball around in a circle, clad in multicolored team uniforms.

Girls, urged on by an array of coaches shouting instructions.

Girls, with freckles and red hair, or long dark hair like Freshta and Laila's, short waves like Miriam's.

Samira stares at a dozen different goalies, rubbing their gloved hands in the cold, diving to divert a dozen different passes.

Where did they all come from?

Then, a tall, strong figure with a thick, dark braid down her back strides across the field. Ariana. She turns, catches sight of them, and stops still.

At that first sight of her, they are happy—excited that she has heard about the tournament too. Now, with her addition, surely they will win.

They hurry over, smiling.

"I can't play on your team," she says quickly.

"Why not?" Laila asks, confused.

"I am injured," Laila will remember Ariana answering.

"She's on another team." A tall man has walked over to them. He has a dark, thin mustache and curly black hair. "Even though her team has been eliminated, she can't play again for another one."

"But she's on *our* team," Freshta says, startled.

"No. Not in this tournament."

He is Abdul Saboor Walizada, tournament organizer and head of the Women's Soccer Committee within the Afghanistan Football Federation.

He asks for their team name, first taking down their ages, names, cell phone numbers.

"Roots of Peace," Freshta says, in English.

"It should be a Dari word," he says as he looks at their

excited faces. He scribbles something down. "I'll put down *Setara.*"

Stars.

"You knew about the tournament. Why didn't you tell us?" Laila demands of Ariana as soon as Walizada walks away. "We are teammates."

"I didn't think you would play," Ariana answers.

"I am your friend," Laila says. "You should have told me."

"I'm sorry," Ariana says, raising her hands. "I'm sorry," she says again and walks away to greet her new teammates.

Robina and Freshta turn their heads away.

"It's okay," Samira murmurs, tugging at Laila's sleeve. "Let's just play."

"No," Laila says tightly. "If you're on our team, then you're on the team. If I just went to another team, how would you feel?"

"Yes, yes," Samira replies uncomfortably. "But now it's time for us to play."

But two teams are already on the field.

"Only one game is played each day. " Walizada has walked over to them again. "Come back tomorrow."

As they shuffle off the field, someone is shouting.

"You can't play here!"

It's a girl from another team.

"You're too late," she says. "You can't join anymore."

"Are you scared?" Freshta yells back.

"No," she responds. "You just can't play with us."

"Why not?"

"You don't have enough girls on your team."

The other teams all field six players—with reserves. Without Ariana, the Stars have only five.

Walizada, who's been watching, intervenes.

"First, you play," he says sternly to the girl. "Then you argue. Everybody can play here."

That night, the five girls gather again at Freshta and Laila's home. Arzo notes their anxious expressions, the way Freshta and Laila throw their bags down. Miriam and Robina are quiet and solemn; Samira darts pained looks between her friends' faces.

"Freshta *jan*, what time is the game tomorrow?" Arzo asks.

"We need to be there before ten A.M.," she answers shortly.

After dinner, the girls retreat to the bedroom. Laila shuts the door, and their talk spills out, overflowing like the water from the bathroom pipes.

They are stunned by Ariana's betrayal. Why hadn't she told them about the tournament? If Halima hadn't suggested they come, they never would have known.

In America, they had pledged themselves to one another.

"We are like sisters," they had said. "So whatever happens, we have to tell each other everything."

Ariana has broken that promise.

"Why did she do this?"

"What did we do to her?"

"Why didn't she tell us?"

"Maybe she had some kind of problem," Freshta suggests. "Maybe we should give her one more chance?"

"Yes," Robina quickly agrees.

The other girls do not know that Ariana had approached Robina secretly several weeks earlier, to recruit her for the tournament.

"Do not tell the others," Ariana had said. "But I hope you will play on my team."

Robina was flattered. Of all the players, Ariana had chosen her for the new team. Ariana trusted her.

But finally, Robina claimed housework the day of the first game. Still, she did not tell her teammates about Ariana's offer.

"Let's give her another chance," Robina repeats to Freshta, Laila, Samira, and Miriam.

All the girls agree. Tomorrow, they will ask Ariana one last time:

Whose team are you on?

far afield

AMERICA, JULY 2004

N THE MORNING of July 7, Barbara and the girls caught a red-eye flight from Washington, D.C., to Hartford, Connecticut. They were headed to the Ethel Walker School, where I'd arranged for their soccer camp to take place. I had come up a few days earlier, leaving right after the Fourth of July Afghan-American Soccer Cup, to finalize the logistics and complete the more mundane tasks like outfitting their rooms with blankets, sheets, and pillows.

I met their plane at Bradley International Airport at 8 A.M. The girls' luggage had increased exponentially. They each arrived dragging yet another bag filled with new clothing and equipment, some purchased, most donated.

For the next three-and-a-half weeks, they were going to be housed at the all-girls Ethel Walker boarding school and continue training in preparation for the International Children's

Games, to be held in Cleveland, July 28 to August 2—the end of their U.S. trip.

As we piled into my parents' green minivan—they'd kindly lent it to me for the duration of the camp—butterflies were fluttering madly in my stomach.

I was scared. The girls were now my responsibility. Barbara would stay only a day. It was up to me to make sure the girls got real training . . . up to me to make sure they were well taken care of.

Now they were here. The previous February, I'd made a list of every boarding school in New England, and then proceeded to call them one by one. There were more than thirty. Many schools were already booked for the summer months. After fifteen unfruitful phone calls, I spoke with Kim Blanchard, an administrative assistant at the Ethel Walker School.

She put me in touch with a local youth soccer coach, Jerry Garlick, who was plugged in to a network of hundreds of coaches across the state. After just one e-mail from him to his colleagues on the Simsbury Soccer Club board, ten local youth soccer coaches volunteered to teach on a rotating basis at the camp.

When we arrived at the campus from the airport, Kim and Jerry were there to greet us. Elegant redbrick buildings, fronted by rows of slender white columns, surrounded a campus of thick lawns and tall, leafy trees.

Kim walked with us to our dorm—a two-story brick building secluded from the main campus. It had a landscaped inner cloister not visible from the outside, with tennis courts that lined the narrow back road.

After I gave them their room assignments, I left the girls

to unpack. They were quiet, which by now was unusual, and seemed uneasy in the vast, echoing space among the rows of locked, empty rooms.

"You'll be fine," I told them, hoping they would be.

LATER, KIM AND Jerry escorted us to one of the school's three soccer fields, at the bottom of a steep knoll behind the gymnasium. Samira, Roya, Ariana, Laila, and Miriam ran down the hill; Freshta, Deena, Robina, and Nadia were in a deep conversation, giggling as they walked.

When we got to the field, the girls split up into two teams. Kim, Jerry, Barbara, and I took seats on the metal stands on the sidelines as they began their game. The brilliant sun lit the lawn to a vibrant jade.

Jerry squinted toward the field, assessing the girls' skills. Suddenly the game came to an abrupt halt. The entire team rushed to the middle of the field, hands flailing, voices raised.

Embarrassed, I hurried out to them.

"What happened?" I asked.

Amid the chaos of shouting voices, I made out that Miriam and Deena had gone for the ball and collided.

"She pushed me!" Miriam announced.

"But you were both fighting for the ball, and sometimes pushing happens," I said, the girls surrounding me. "It's not on purpose," I assured her.

Miriam frowned, thinking about my words and considering the possibility that Deena hadn't pushed her deliberately.

She didn't buy it. Miriam pointed to Deena again, demanding an explanation for the collision.

What do I do now? Pushing and shoving is part of soccer; didn't the girls know that? To be competitive, players needed to be able to fight intensely for the ball, to make a goal and defend the net. But to these girls, ordinary parts of the game became personal affronts, a purposeful act intended to hurt. Soon I would come to understand what was beneath their reactions.

I decided it best to call it quits, and we all went back to the dorm.

Instead of four to a room as they'd had at Barbara's, here each girl had only one or two roommates. I'd placed Laila and Ariana together; both were quiet and easygoing.

Miriam and Deena were in the second room. I had hoped Deena's cheery, gentle personality would soothe Miriam's quick hurts. Now, after their argument, I wondered if it would work.

Nadia, Samira, and Roya would share the triple. Perhaps Samira's intensity would be balanced with Nadia's humor, I reasoned, and Roya went well with everyone.

Robina and Freshta were left to the final assigned room. Throughout the previous two weeks they had quarreled and squabbled but by now I hoped they would be able to get along.

I had my hand on the door to my room when Barbara stopped me in the hall. "How do you think it is going, Awista?"

"Well, this is all new to them. It will work out, I think," I said, praying that it would.

"Of course it will," she said.

As I began to unpack, I heard banging and clanging from down the hall.

I rushed into the hallway. In all four rooms, the girls were dismantling their bunk beds and shoving the frames together on the floor. I laughed with relief. Of course! None of them had ever slept in a bunk bed before.

Miriam saw me. "We don't want to fall down, Awista jan."

⁂

DURING THE NEXT three weeks, the girls' soccer skills improved. Coaches from the first few practices who returned two weeks later were surprised at how much better they had become.

"They're very committed to learning the sport," said one of the coaches. "I can only imagine how important this is to them."

To balance out the grueling and demanding practices, I included non-soccer activities in the daily routine: baking, tie-dying T-shirts, and face painting. I even organized a "science day."

Friends from General Electric, my former employer, planned that day well. The girls made silly putty (glue, water, and borax), folded origami cranes, and painted clay figures. Most exciting was constructing a volcano from clay and then making it erupt.

"Thank yooouu, thank you very much," said Deena to one of the GE instructors.

"Thank yooouu, thank you very much," echoed Nadia.

The two girls had learned their first English phrase, and would use it creatively whenever they thought it might apply.

Like most summer camps in the U.S., the Ethel Walker School had a dining hall with typical "camp" food. Surprisingly, all the girls chose food mainly from the salad bar. Laila loved hard-boiled eggs; Ariana and Deena ate bowlfuls of spaghetti with marinara sauce.

Other groups also used the campus, but we stood out. Each day we wore our team practice shirts, either in red or yellow, with huge numbers on the back. We'd all sit together in wooden chairs at the long table as we ate.

The cafeteria workers adored the girls, especially Deena and Nadia with their distinctive "Thank yooouu, thank you very much."

A former GE colleague of mine donated nine bikes for the girls to have for the summer, and soon bike riding became their favorite post-soccer activity. I borrowed a bicycle from one of the coaches, and joined them in exploring the bucolic school grounds, as we rode up and down the well-maintained paths.

One afternoon, after riding around the entire campus, we drew close to the dormitory and saw my mother speaking with Kim.

"*Khala jan!*" Miriam and Laila called out.

"*Salaam,*" my mother said, waving.

We parked our bikes near her car. "*Mor,* how nice to see you," I said. "I wasn't expecting you to come today."

"I wanted to watch the girls' practice. Oh, and I have something for them."

She went to the car and brought out a shopping bag. She drew out eight composition books, each one neatly printed with the name of one of the girls on the cover. "This is for you," she told them. "For your English."

Inside the books were the English alphabet and some basic phrases—"Hello," "Good-bye," "What time is it?" and the ubiquitous "Thank you."

"You can rewrite the words, so you can practice your English," my mother told them.

"*Tashakor, khala jan,*" each girl said as she took a book and pressed it against her chest.

◦◦◦

EACH DAY, EACH week seemed to bring something new. What didn't change, however, was the girls' constant squabbling. Practice sessions became a testing ground.

Two weeks into camp, the girls played a friendly game against one another. After Laila scored a goal, Robina came up to her.

"Why didn't you pass the ball to me? Didn't you see that I was open?" Robina demanded. "I could have scored the goal!"

I was flabbergasted. I thought they understood: A goal scored represented a team effort.

My years of team sports at the high school and university level had taught me that, yes, teammates sometimes clashed and that virtually everyone wanted to be the one who scored. But this level of arguing was in another league. The frequency and intensity of the girls' fights was something I'd never seen before. I couldn't understand it.

Why? I asked myself for the hundredth time. I'd watch

the girls in the field: Robina's fierceness, Laila's defensive stance, the rest of the girls in a circle tensed and ready.

Then it clicked.

These children, thirteen- and fourteen-year-olds for the most part, had spent their entire lives in a country at *war*. They woke up each day wondering if it would be their last. *Will a bomb drop near my home? Will a bullet hit me today? Will my family have to flee from our home?*

When had they ever seen conflict resolved calmly?

The girls were passionate to be sure, and that would serve them well. But passion without direction is a rudderless ship. Could I help them navigate their way to becoming a team?

I phoned my mother. Again.

The next day my mother stopped by again on her way home from work. She is a short woman, with short, curly hair and hazel eyes specked with amber. That day she wore white linen slacks with a flowered top—large white hibiscuses on a black background. I remember her pearl earrings and matching necklace.

My mother always smiles. Always. She arrived with a covered dish, *raut,* an Afghan cake, the girls' favorite. By this time she'd witnessed the girls playing soccer, plus they'd been to our home twice. All the girls felt comfortable with her.

I was glad to see her.

"Do you want me to speak with the girls in the common room?" she asked.

"Yes, *Mor,* sit them down there all together. That way you won't be choosing one girl's room over another's."

Just then, seven of the girls came careening around the corner on their bikes. Robina and Deena had stayed behind and were sitting on the wide steps leading to the dorm entrance.

My mother smiled. "Come, let us all go inside," she said in Dari.

The girls came up to her, kissing her one by one with three alternative pecks on the cheeks. I watched as the youngsters circled her, their faces lit up.

"I want to speak with you girls," she told them in Dari.

I stood outside, near the window.

I felt a familiar pang. Outside, dusk was falling. Crickets began their constant seesaw chatter. I looked around at the campus, the verdant panorama. I had brought the girls here. I had found the camp. Found the trainers, coaches. Eight months of work, yet still the gulf between them and me was wide. Sometimes I felt the distance between us so keenly, it felt insurmountable.

Later, my mother would repeat the conversation to me. She had the girls sit down in the chairs and couches in the dorm's common room.

"While you are here, you are a family. You have to learn to get along, trust each other, and work together, *famidi?*" Understand?

"Yes, together, *Khala jan*," they murmured.

"You cannot fight with each other. *Famidi?*"

Nine pair of eyes were glued to the floor. They were embarrassed, now that they saw their behavior through the eyes of an elder whom they loved and respected.

"We will be good," Robina whispered. Everyone nodded.

In the days that followed, I overheard girls saying "sorry" after bumping into each other on the field.

"It's okay," the other would respond.

❦

ONE WEEK BEFORE the International Children's Games were to begin in Cleveland, and after weeks of practice, we had our first scrimmage since the July Fourth Afghan-American Soccer Cup. It was an evening game, organized by Vaughn Robbins, a local coach. He'd selected a team of younger eleven- to thirteen-year-old girls from Simsbury who he felt were about equal to the size and skill of the Afghan players.

The night before the match the girls kept to their usual pregame routine and laid their uniforms out carefully, checking and rechecking their equipment.

The next day they ate their lunch in silence. The girls were being challenged to push toward another level. I was glad the game was being held on the campus, where the terrain was familiar.

Naturally there was worry—and doubt. But those feelings dissipated when the game started. Their aggressive pressure on the ball and Samira's quick hands on goal became an impenetrable defense that held the other team at bay. By the end of the first half, the girls had pulled off a scoreless tie.

Then the second half began. The first goal scored against them was like a bag tearing; the form the girls had held through the first half burst apart, scattering them across the field. The offense unraveled, positions disintegrated. They ran recklessly, forgetting directions and their training.

It was as if they'd lost their bearings. The only clear position left on the field was Samira's, the goalie. But finally it became too much for her also. She tore off her goalie gloves and ran upfield, too frustrated to keep still. Then she saw her mistake, and backtracked frantically when the other team swiped the ball and drove forward. Minutes later they scored another goal, followed soon by yet another.

"How much time's left?" Miriam panted as she ran past me, obviously hoping the answer would be none.

A lifetime later, the final whistle blew. Robina and Laila had both scored in the waning minutes, but it wasn't enough. We lost 4–2.

The two teams met at the center of the field, lined up, and shook hands. The Afghan girls trudged back to the sidelines where I was standing.

Tears poured down their faces.

They'd never lost before.

But I knew, absolutely knew, that these girls would make a difference—in the sport, in their country, and for themselves—if they could only learn to trust one another.

a team of their own

ARIANA, KABUL, DECEMBER 2005

"However tall the mountain, there's always a road."
—AFGHAN PROVERB

W HEN ARIANA RETURNS to Kabul that August, she eagerly rejoins her teammates from the American trip at their weekly Friday practice.

Her first action is to assign herself on offense. In America coaches placed her on defense, against her objections. They said that her strength and size made her perfect to stay back and protect the net.

But she wanted to score goals, not prevent them.

No matter how many times she was assured of its importance, defense required long stretches of time standing still, waiting to react to someone else's initiative.

Her height gave Ariana perspective across the pitch,

enabling her to see, but not participate in, what was happening on the field.

The few times she was allowed to play offense, in Cleveland and Connecticut, confirmed her feeling. She longed to move, to run, to score, to be with the ball, always.

Now, in Afghanistan, it is time to stop playing defense.

She is ready to go on offense.

❧ ❦ ❧

THE ALL-GIRLS HIGH school that Ariana attends is a five-minute walk from her house. In the afternoons, she watches girls training for volleyball and basketball on the grounds outside the school. They don't play soccer. But, after competing against international teams in America, soccer is all Ariana wants to play.

She approaches one of the sports teachers.

"Are there any soccer teams?"

"No," the teacher says. "But if you want to play basketball or volleyball, you can come."

Ariana shakes her head. These are the traditional sports played by girls in Afghanistan; soccer is a sport reserved for men. But she has decided it is time for that to change.

"I'm trying to start girls' soccer," she says with a polite smile, and leaves.

She is not the only one with that goal. Across the city, at Ghazi Stadium, the Afghanistan Football Federation (AFF) has been independently working on the same idea.

Formed in 1933, the AFF joined the Fédération Internationale de Football Association (FIFA), soccer's international governing body, in 1948. It was a founding member of the Asian Football Confederation six years later, in 1954.

But when the Soviet war started, virtually all of Afghanistan's sports programs came under siege. In 1984, the men's soccer team played its last international match for almost twenty years. When the Taliban came to power in 1996, they stopped girls from competing in any sport and outlawed men's boxing.

In 1999, the International Olympic Committee (IOC) banned Afghanistan from competing in the Olympic Games, citing the prohibitions against women athletes as a major factor.

When the Taliban left Kabul, Afghanistan reentered the world sports stage. In 2002, the men's soccer team competed at the Asian Games in Busan. They were outscored during the tournament 32–0—but it was a beginning.

A year later, AFF approved a new $610,000 plan to rebuild their national soccer program, sponsored by FIFA, the Asian Football Conference, and the German, English, and Iranian Football Associations. The plan covered everything from youth soccer to building a new infrastructure, strategy, and administration. "Technical development" received 13 percent of the budget—including the establishment of the first women's soccer program in Afghanistan's history.

As the federation leadership reassessed the organization's structure and administration in the spring of 2004, a former national team player applied for a position on the Youth Committee.

Abdul Saboor Walizada had dreamed about playing for the national team as a child in Kabul, as did millions of

Afghan boys. Like them, he grew up playing pickup soccer in the streets and parks near his house and eagerly following the exploits of the national team. On game days, he and his father joined thousands of devoted fans filling Ghazi Stadium, where they cheered on their national heroes.

Walizada's dream came true. He was selected for the men's national team. During his ten years on the team he would earn a reputation as a fierce defender who used his head—physically and intellectually—on the field. He loved defense.

After retiring from playing, Walizada worked within the federation training boys in soccer. By 2003, he was eager to continue instructing Afghanistan's aspiring athletes in the revamped federation, shaping the sports system.

When AFF announced its management teams in 2004, Walizada was stunned. His request to join the new Youth Committee had been turned down.

He'd been selected to helm a different program—the inaugural Women's Soccer Committee.

Walizada had nothing against girls playing soccer. But he had no interest in training them. The idea of girls playing soccer was controversial enough—but to be trained by a man? He wanted nothing to do with it.

Privately, he took members of the selection panel aside.

"Why did you elect me to this position?" he asked each of them.

"You've taught in schools and trained players with no experience. You know how to interact with students and with the beginners."

Walizada listed his objections. There were many.

"How can I, as a man, go to girls' schools and convince teachers and parents to allow their girls to be part of the soccer team?"

Each panel member repeated the same refrain: We have confidence in your ability to do the job.

He moved on to his second point.

"In our society and our environment, it is not acceptable for a woman to play soccer!"

He admitted he did not personally agree with this statement, but many people did—and *they* would cause difficulties.

Then there was the matter of security.

"Families won't be willing to send their daughters out to play in the field. Even the federation offices are not safe. How can I gain the confidence of families to trust me with their daughters?" he persisted.

Men had coached women's sports in Kabul during the 1970s. But not since then.

"How will I convince them? How do we prove, Allah forbid, we aren't taking them to inappropriate places, like a park or the cinema?"

"This job," the panel finally admitted, "is the only one you are being offered within the federation."

Walizada accepted.

The Federation paired him with Shamsi Hayat, the director of the women's programs for Afghanistan's National Olympic Committee. She had been charged with developing a comprehensive women's sports program, with the aim of earning Afghanistan's reentry to the Olympic movement. That summer, they succeeded. Afghanistan sent five athletes to the 2004 games in Athens, including its first two female representatives, who competed in judo and track and field.

Shamsi had been working on establishing basketball, volleyball, table tennis, and other sports before the federation asked her to help Walizada pursue the girls' soccer program.

First, they created a list of girls' high schools in Kabul. In many cases, Shamsi knew a teacher or two at the school from her other recruiting efforts. She'd call them up and talk about soccer, its benefits, and the burgeoning program. If the teacher agreed, then a meeting would be arranged with the principal.

At each school, Shamsi and Walizada faced a barrage of questions.

Should girls be playing soccer at all?

What would they wear?

Why was Walizada, a man, their coach?

Patiently, they explained the health benefits of soccer; the modest clothes that would cover the girls' legs and arms, the caps over their hair. Walizada agreed that a woman coach would be better—but there were none trained.

Some of the school principals listened carefully and agreed to connect them with interested students. But more than half refused.

When the school principals refused to allow their students to join the team, Walizada and Shamsi would sometimes approach the teachers instead, asking them to help arrange private meetings with parents.

The two of them would visit the homes of the girls they sought and speak with the mothers and fathers directly.

"There are no female trainers qualified to teach girls," Shamsi told the parents frankly. "But all of our colleagues—male and female—have full trust in Walizada."

Even so, there would always be a woman present. They would train at Ghazi Stadium, which was well guarded. Practices would always take place within the secure confines of the stadium and under scrupulous supervision.

They reiterated the health benefits of soccer—more running than volleyball, less physical contact than basketball.

As Shamsi and Walizada scoured schools for players, they found an additional lead that seemed promising. The local TV station had recently run a story about a group of girls who had traveled to America to learn soccer. As Walizada watched interviews with the girls, it was clear to him that they now had a level of training beyond any girl in Afghanistan.

But he did not know how to reach them.

꧁✿꧂

A FEW DAYS later, Walizada's cell phone rings.

"*Salaam,*" says a voice. "My name is Ariana. Is this the women's soccer program?"

She got his number from a neighbor, Ariana explains. She just returned from training in America—and wants to play soccer.

"I was trying to find you!" Walizada exclaims. "Why don't you come to Ghazi Stadium and we can talk further?"

Ariana hangs up and runs inside, to her mother.

"*Madar,*" she shouts. "Tomorrow I'm going to the Olympics!"

Afghanistan's National Olympic Committee has established its offices in Ghazi Stadium, located on the Sarak Masjid Eid Gah or the Road of the Eid Gah Mosque. Since its construction in 1923, the stadium has served as the country's national stadium, hosting Afghanistan's first international soccer match in 1941, a 0–0 tie against Iran.

For decades, it hosted Afghanistan's largest soccer tournaments and public events. When the Taliban were driven from Kabul, the city celebrated by resurrecting the banned game of *buzkashi,* Afghanistan's ancient national sport. Thousands flooded into the stadium to cheer on horsemen bravely riding their horses in competition to score goals.

Ariana has seen Ghazi Stadium on television, covered in a news segment after the Taliban left Kabul. After more than twenty years of war, its seats have been destroyed, the grass shredded, exposing streaks of dust, garbage, and papers piled all over the field. What would she find there now?

One hour and two buses later, Ariana arrives at the stadium, seven miles from her home in Khayr Khana. An armed guard emerges. Barbed wire coils along the top of the walls.

"Who are you?" the guard asks, blocking her entrance. "Where are you going?"

"I'm here to speak with someone from the soccer federation."

"There are no girls playing soccer here."

"I'm here to see *ustad* Walizada, the coach."

With a skeptical look, he lets her through.

She steps into the dark, cool corridors of the stadium. She doesn't know where to go. Nervously, she fumbles inside her purse and pulls out her cell phone.

"*Salaam,* this is Ariana," she tells Walizada. "I just arrived at the stadium. Where should I meet you?"

"Wait there," he says. A minute later, he bounds downstairs, a broad smile on his face.

They head to his office. Ariana shares her desire to compete as a soccer player.

"We need more girls like you!" he commends her. "If you want to start a team at your school—I will come anytime you are ready and teach them."

His office window overlooks the massive field, which Ariana sees is blanketed in green, with stands arranged in clean, neat rows. Boys and girls are training in separate corners of the field, girls practicing sprints as the boys scrimmage at soccer.

"Where did the killing take place?" Ariana asks him, curious.

He points to the center of the field.

"Right there," he says.

It seemed like a plain playing field but here it was, the place she had seen on TV—the woman crumbling to the ground. She shakes her head.

Walizada interrupts her thought. "Please tell the other girls from your American trip to come next time too," he says.

As he leads her out the door she promises.

"I will tell them."

· · ·

Ariana returns to the Roots of Peace field that Friday, a few days later. It feels smaller than she remembered. Later, Ariana will assert that she extended Walizada's invitation to her teammates—that she shared his vision for a network of girls' teams across Afghanistan.

"He is a professional player," she remembers telling them. "And he will teach us. There may even be a national team that might one day compete in the Olympic Games!"

"My family won't let me," she recalls Miriam saying.

"We are too busy with school," the rest of the girls responded. "This is enough."

AMONG HER EIGHT teammates from the American trip, Ariana was the oldest. Early on, she became someone the girls turned to.

When Nadia nervously announced she had a headache on the plane, Ariana comforted her.

"Don't worry," she said soothingly. "I will tell the pilot to stop the plane."

"Really?"

"Yes."

Nadia narrowed her eyes, then laughed.

"No," she said. "I know you're joking."

Ariana shrugged and smiled.

The game was everything to Ariana. The girls played everywhere; in the backyard of Barbara's house, in parks, even at the Pentagon.

Only two weeks after they arrived the team was invited to play at the Pentagon, where they were met by then Secretary of Defense Donald Rumsfeld—and a handful of professional women's soccer players.

Two teams were formed, mixing the professional women with the girls.

When the women passed her the ball, Ariana struggled to catch it with her foot and bring it under control. She couldn't run at their pace, match their speed, sustain their endurance.

I'm not like them. I'm just a simple girl.

But as they skimmed across the grass, she realized the real difference between them: They had been practicing for more than a decade, on grass fields, with real goals, a supply of balls, and constant coaching. *We just got here,* Ariana thought.

The most amazing thing, though, was that the professional players didn't always shoot, even when they could.

In Afghanistan, Ariana had always resisted giving up the ball to anyone, always seized the chance to score herself. All of them had. But these players, more powerful than any of them, held back, shared the ball, built a play with a series of small, sure passes that advanced them forward.

They didn't teach her any specific skills that day. But Ariana learned.

❧

IN KABUL, ARIANA returns to the stadium to practice every spare moment. On her second visit, Walizada gives her a tour. New grass has been laid down and the open-air, concrete VIP box refurbished, replete with brown leather couches. President Karzai sits there to view matches and to address audiences during the National Parade.

Ariana and Walizada walk down to the field. Twenty girls are racing one another.

"Here," Walizada says, handing Ariana a soccer ball. "Play."

She grins and runs onto the field, dribbling up and down the sidelines, practicing her soccer before thousands of empty seats.

The track-and-field players see Ariana running drills by herself.

"Why don't you come run with us?" they yell over.

"Why don't you join *me*?" Ariana calls back.

"There are many of us—and you're alone."

Ariana shrugs.

"I prefer soccer."

She continues her dribbling. The men's soccer team begins practice. The boys glance at her. They have never seen a girl playing soccer here before. Ariana stops and walks to the sidelines, where she can observe their techniques.

A ball skitters out of bounds. Ariana leaps up to retrieve it. She dribbles it skillfully back to the boys, who are bemused, watching her.

"Can I have one pass, please?" she asks them, with a confident smile, sending the ball back with a deft, hard kick.

The boys look at one another. One of them lopes forward to corral the pass, cupping it with the side of his foot. He hesitates, then lifts his leg and chips the ball back to her. She stops it with her foot and drives back a clean, straight pass.

"Oh," says the boy. "You know how to play."

She joins their circle, passing and kicking the ball around until the boys decide it has been enough.

"Okay," one says, not unkindly. "Now go."

Not all the boys are as understanding. As the weeks progress, some taunt Ariana.

"You're a girl. Don't come every day."

"Why aren't you like the other girls?"

Other insinuations are more serious.

"Do you like the boys who come here?" asks one of the players. For a woman in Kabul, this can be a damaging statement. One cannot be too forward.

One day, Ariana is running laps around the field and after just a few minutes, she stops, tired. One of the boys nearby bursts into laughter.

"You don't have the energy to play!"

Ariana glares back at him.

"Leave it," he says, shaking his head. "Soccer's not a sport for girls."

Ariana has had enough.

"Why?" she asks, advancing on him. "You have two eyes, a nose, and so do I."

He looks back at her, confused.

"You have two legs, so do I. The energy that you have, I have also—but I need practice. You've practiced a lot because you could, anytime you want. But I'm a girl. I can't leave my house and go practice anytime I want. That's all I need. But if I practiced hard, I could play against you. Our games would be equal."

"Maybe you can play with me," he says, eyes lowered. He wants the conversation to end.

But now she is on a roll, pressing forward, attacking.

"If all people talk like you, then we'll be stopped. But if you encourage girls like me, saying 'Yes, very good,' then we will practice and we will be good soccer players in the future. The world will know Afghanistan is a country that can compete with anyone."

"Oh, leave it," he mutters. "Okay?"

"If you don't like me," Ariana says, "well, I don't like you either."

She stalks off the field.

Walizada watches Ariana absorb these attacks, block them, send them back with a quick response. He knows what it is like to play defense—you can repel the shots, but they leave a bruise.

He takes her aside.

"People say things," he tells her, and shrugs. "I know these guys are like your father, your brothers. If you want to continue, don't leave."

"I'm fine," Ariana tells him.

She wants to continue. Nothing will stop her.

NOW ARIANA GOES to Ghazi Stadium almost every afternoon. After a few weeks, two or three other girls start appearing, drawn there by Walizada and Shamsi. Their mothers come with them at first, to watch them practice.

A small tournament is scraped together among five or six teams, drawing handfuls of girls from schools across the city.

Ariana competes with her new team.

Ariana likes these teammates. They are smaller and a few years younger than she is, quiet and awed by her size and her skill. When Walizada is not there to direct them, Ariana leads the practices.

When Ariana tells them to run, they run. When she tells them to line up and start passing, they form pairs and send the ball back and forth. When she announces that it's time for shooting, they run to form a line in front of the goal.

They call themselves *Atma,* the Only One.

In December 2005, after nearly a year of training and competing in small tournaments, with teams from other schools, Walizada takes Ariana aside.

He is planning another tournament, this time not just for practice.

"We're ready," he tells her. "It's time to form a national team."

on the road

AMERICA, JULY–AUGUST 2004

OUR IN THE morning is never a good time to get up. Deena and Nadia, usually perky, were crabby. Samira barked about life being "unfair." The rest of the crew hauled their luggage like it was weighted with lead.

Robina, as usual, was coordinating and checking that no one had left anything in the drawers or dressers. Ariana was still in front of the mirror, dickering with her hair. Miriam was crouched in the hallway, her bags at her feet, eyes closed, leaning against the wall.

We were up at this unearthly hour to catch a flight to Cleveland. The girls were now going to enter the world of competitive soccer: The International Children's Games. The Games originated in 1968 in what was then Slovenia, Yugoslavia, starting out with nine towns in Europe participating.

Since then, it had grown to include delegations from more than seventy countries.

The evening before, we'd said good-bye to Roya. There was a great deal of sobbing, arms thrown around her, sworn promises that they would all meet again.

Roya had been an anchor for us all. Her translating skills had improved, and by now she could almost speak Dari and English in the same breath. But more than that, her joyful enthusiasms, her experience playing soccer, and her knowledge of American ways had made the Afghan girls' stay richer.

"I'll miss you all," she told them. "Good luck in Cleveland!"

"*Tashakor,* Roya!" they chorused.

Once we arrived in Cleveland, we headed to our dorm rooms at John Carroll University, the host site for the Children's Games. The Jesuit-run school was located in University Heights, its sixty-acre suburban campus only ten miles east of downtown Cleveland.

The girls hastily unpacked, picked up two soccer balls, and by unspoken agreement, quickly made their way outside to scrimmage on the lawn.

We spent the rest of the day adjusting to our new dorm and reviewing our busy schedule of practices and games. Tired from the day's travel, we went right to sleep.

Early the next morning, we discovered Ali Kazemaini waiting for us outside the front door of the university. "*Salaam* to you all. I'm Ali. I'm your coach for the Games."

He stared long and hard at each member of the team. "Remember," he said in a stern voice, "you must have fun!"

An Iranian-American, Ali was head coach of the men's soccer team at John Carroll, and he soon had the eight girls running plays on the varsity field. They were thrilled to have a coach for the Games, and now they had one with whom they could easily communicate. Ali spoke English of course, but also Farsi, which stems from the same ancient Persian root as Dari.

I would understand enough, I supposed, if only through everyone's body language and Ali's translations.

"It's great that you're doing this," I told him.

"Soccer's for everyone," he answered with enthusiasm. He turned his attention to the field.

"Be aware. Watch out for each other," he bellowed. "Stay in your positions."

Samira, at the goal, clapped her hands.

"Teamwork, teamwork" she yelled in Dari.

"Teamwork," I yelled in Pashto.

"Teamwork," Ariana echoed in English.

❧❧❧

ON FRIDAY EVENING, we prepared for the Opening Ceremonies of the Games. Dressed in matching pink khaki pants, pink hats, light green T-shirts, and white zip-up fleece jackets, the girls and I rode a bus to Cleveland Browns Stadium. There, hundreds of young athletes milled around, waiting for the upcoming walk through the city streets. The parade ended at the City Green on Lakeside Avenue, which had been turned into a "Festival Village" for the Games.

An official blew the whistle. Afghanistan was the first country alphabetically. We were to lead the march.

Following the organizers, we moved forward into the warm summer air and onto the wide streets of downtown Cleveland. Ariana was the designated team captain, and she brandished the large black, red, and green Afghanistan flag as it snapped in the wind. Robina, Miriam, Deena, Laila, Freshta, Samira, and Nadia lined up in pairs and a three-some behind her, holding hands and waving to the throngs of cheering adults and children who lined both sides of the streets. I walked behind them with my sister Zohra, who had joined us on the trip.

I could hear the buzz sweeping through the crowd as we passed: "Those girls are from Afghanistan!" The country had never participated in the Children's Games before. People craned their necks to see us. The girls were relaxed, their faces bright, as they laughed and waved back to the crowd.

I was reminded of the reaction we'd received at the Fourth of July Soccer Cup. But this time the cheers were from Americans. The local press would use the word "enam-ored" to describe their welcome of us.

Afghanistan was announced. The eight girls climbed the stage at Festival Village to roaring applause.

"Did you hear the crowd, Awista *jan*?" Miriam said excit-edly later that evening. Deena and Nadia were parading around the room, imitating their earlier march.

Ariana was beaming. "You saw how they greeted the flag?" she asked.

"Yes, you carried it well," I said.

We were in the small common room off the entrance of the college.

"It was for all of you, each one of you," I told them.

"And you too, Awista *jan,*" Robina added.

I swallowed and held back my tears of pride. These youngsters had worked hard—on and off the field—and it had finally paid off.

They'd become a team.

The next morning, I knocked on each of the girls' doors. They were paired two to a room, and everyone was pleased with the arrangements. On the outside of all the doors was a small slot and tag announcing which country the athletes were from. On the girls' doors, and mine, it proclaimed "Afghanistan."

Ali had arranged a practice session before the afternoon game, their first official match. Robina, as usual, was already up and would make sure everyone was ready.

I turned around to go back to my room. In addition to the tags with country of origin, outside each room was a white-board for messages. Scribbled across mine was a childish drawing of a plane heading for two tall buildings.

I entered my dorm room and closed the door. Sitting on the edge of the bed, I exhaled slowly.

ON SEPTEMBER 11, 2001, I was the only Afghan-American student at the University of Rochester.

That Tuesday morning, I had just finished an assignment for my chemistry class. As I gathered up my notes, a listener phoned in to the radio station I had been absently listening to as I studied.

"A plane has crashed into the World Trade Center!"

"What?" stammered the announcer, "What are you talking about?"

The caller repeated what he'd said.

I heard it, but it didn't compute. I flicked the radio off and hurried across the large campus to make my 9:30 A.M. grad-level chemistry lecture. As I arrived, no one was yet talking about the news. After the lecture, I handed in my assignment and went to the library, intent on putting in a few hours of work. On the way, threads of conversations flew around the lawn:

"A plane."

"World Trade Center."

"Terrorists."

Without totally realizing it, I had emerged into a different world.

I went to the library, straight to a computer. Saw the video.

This can't be happening.

During the next few days, I watched in horror along with the whole country as the film footage was replayed over and over. My initial shock became grief, then fear. Blasted across newspapers around the world were searing words: Taliban. Training camps. Afghanistan.

The same country unraveled by decades of war was now a target for the world. None of the hijackers was Afghan, but the news reports said they had been trained in Afghanistan. *In my homeland.*

Muslims were being singled out and attacked across the

country, even in Rochester, New York. A man had been attacked coming out of a grocery store. It turned out he was actually a Sikh, wearing a turban.

I phoned my father. "I am nervous here, *Baba*. I think I should come home."

"No, Awista. You need to focus and study. That's what you need. It will be fine," he said. "You must finish this year."

My father's response made me realize that my own response was too emotional. So I stayed.

Few people at the university knew I was Afghan-American. It wasn't that I was ashamed or defensive about my nationality. I just felt that it was private and, moreover, that it was unimportant. I wanted people to know me just for me. Wasn't that enough?

Throughout my life, my Afghan identity had come alive largely within the safe confines of home. When I went away to college, my connection to the culture grew more distant over the years. Even in the weekly Sunday phone calls home, I spoke less and less Pashto. I was losing the language.

After the incident with the Sikh at the grocery store, I was in the library studying, and a Sikh student sat down near my table. I looked up. I didn't know his name but had seen him around campus.

"How *are* you?" I asked, the same question everyone was asking one another now.

"As well as possible," he answered, looking me in the eye. "Just a few 'Why don't you go back homes.'"

"I know," I said. "I know."

How terribly ironic, I thought. Here I was the Afghan,

but unlike the Sikh student wearing his *dastar,* or head wrap, I didn't wear a *hijab,* or any other traditional garb. I blended in.

Even so, like him, I felt anger, frustration, and, like him, I was afraid.

American friends who knew I was Afghan-American, while being supportive, thought I was being a bit "sensitive."

"This isn't about you, or your country, Awista. This is awful for everyone."

But at night, in my dorm room on the first floor, I lay awake imagining the window breaking, someone's hand coming through, or simply a stone being thrown, shattering the glass.

I first fell in love with sports while watching Olympic ice hockey on TV during the 1994 Winter Games. I sat transfixed as players flew across the ice with grace, speed, and toughness.

From then on, I'd get up at 6 A.M. to watch *SportsCenter* on ESPN, often viewing the same half-hour show two, sometimes three, times in a row. On nights when I controlled the remote—authority that rotated daily among my two siblings, Hiwad and Zohra, and myself—I'd tune in to anything sports-related, much to the dismay of my sister and brother.

But life-changing events make for life-changing decisions. I didn't know it at the time, but like so many fellow citizens in the aftermath of 9/11, I felt the need to *do* something.

THE IDEA MATERIALIZED on a cool May morning.

Images of Afghanistan played like a movie reel in my head; people yearning for peace, young children hungering for their own destiny.

Girls. I began scribbling away on a yellow pad. *Girls. Hmm,* I thought, *how about a sports camp for young female athletes? And as part of it, why don't I sponsor a trip for girls from Afghanistan to the U.S.?*

Starting in the fall of 2003, I worked for eight months straight on what I was optimistically calling the Afghan Youth Sports Exchange (AYSE)—a plan to bring Afghan girls, for six weeks, to the United States, where they'd train intensively in a sport. The trip would culminate with the team competing as Afghanistan's representative in the International Children's Games.

I set up a Web site, telephoned prospective sponsors, and worked on the project proposal. The first organization that supported the project was the New York–based Afghan nonprofit the Afghan Communicator.

I was twenty-three, energetic and eager, inexperienced enough to be audacious.

There was one question, though: Which sport?

I came of age as Julie Foudy and Mia Hamm led the U.S. National Team to two Olympic gold medals, one silver medal, and two FIFA Women's World Cup Championships. Women's soccer had become so popular that the 1999 Women's World Cup final between the U.S. and China had one of the largest TV audiences for any soccer game.

Soccer seemed the best idea for me, I thought. Besides being a gender-neutral sport, it had the advantage of being relatively easy to organize. All the girls would need was a ball and some open space—or so I imagined.

What I didn't know was that there had never, ever, been a girls' soccer team in Afghanistan. The difficulty in finding girls who were playing it, I would later come to understand, wasn't based, as I'd assumed, on the dislocations of war. While girls did play basketball and volleyball, soccer was the game of men.

Call it naïveté, but I didn't fully appreciate how my project would challenge Afghanistan's assumptions about female athletes, putting a group of young Kabul girls at the center of a struggle for acceptance—a struggle that continues today.

13

stars

KABUL, DECEMBER 2005

*"I am a member of a team, and I rely on the team, I defer
to it and sacrifice for it, because the team, not the
individual, is the ultimate champion."*

—MIA HAMM

EFORE THE SUN rises the Sunday of their first tournament since returning from America, Robina stirs awake on her *toshak*. Cold has seeped into the room. Robina looks at the darkened mounds of her teammates sleeping beside her and she feels a surge of excitement. Game Day.

She nudges the other girls awake through the thick tangle of blankets they've pulled around their bodies. Freshta grunts and Laila tugs the covers over her head.

"*Bedar shoo,*" Wake up, Robina says. "We have a game."

She kneels, and together the girls pray as the light filters through the window. They eat a hasty breakfast of *chay* and *halwa,* cooked rice flour spiced with cardamom, sugar, raisins, and slivers of almonds. Then, pulling long winter coats over their new blue-and-black striped uniforms, they file out the door and set off for the field.

Hindu Kush Field is in Koti Sangi, about a mile and a half away from Freshta and Laila's house. Snow covers the ground. The girls walk together, their uniforms visible under their coats, since there won't be a place to change once they arrive.

It is cold. With each breath they feel the cold piercing into their chests, throats, noses.

As they walk past the police station, they are making plans. *What should we do if we can't hear each other on the field? How can we dribble or pass away when somebody's blocking us?* They devise secret ways to communicate without revealing their real intentions to the other team. Laila will shout out Robina's name, but with a signal that she intends to pass to Freshta. Once or twice a game they will use this trick, faking out the other team.

Bullet holes, broken roofs, and smashed-in walls mar many of the houses they pass. Other homes are perfectly intact, multistoried structures with stones that are smooth and cream-colored. Boys are playing in the street.

As the girls pass by, they shout.

"Wow, they're playing sports," one of the boys calls with a smirk, catching sight of their uniforms. "It's not good for them."

"They're becoming boys."

"How can they play—what if their shirts come up?"

The sisters' eleven-year-old brother, Abdullah, has come with them. When the boys start shouting things at the girls, he scowls and shouts back, "Would you say those things to your sister too?"

The boys quiet. The girls keep planning strategy for the game.

The field is a stretch of dusty ground. Snow has been cleared away. A thin spread of trees edges the space, some sporting full foliage, others stripped bare by the cold December air.

Teams are practicing, warming up, and being drilled by coaches in preparation for the day's games.

The girls have one last thing to resolve. They approach Ariana, standing on the sidelines.

"We've decided to give you one more chance," Freshta says, speaking for all of them. "Will you come back to our team?"

"I can't," she says. "I have my own team now."

"Since when?"

"A year ago."

Stunned, they turn and walk away.

Expecting Ariana to finally join them as the sixth player on the team, they hadn't planned to find extra players. It was too late now; Walizada would make an exception this time to let them play with only five, but if they advanced to the final two games of the tournament, they needed to field six players—no exception.

· · ·

The Stars take positions on the field. The other teams and assorted spectators warm to the slight, slender girls. They spread out on the field. They are disciplined enough to avoid the lure of the ball, unlike other teams drawn by its magnetic pull.

"*Setara!*" the crowd shouts, as they backpedal to their positions after each goal. "Stars!"

They emerge, victorious, winning the first game 3–0. Freshta, Robina, and Laila have each scored one goal. Ariana comes over, offering congratulations. No one will speak to her.

The Stars pull on their coats, hug one another. They have made it to the next round.

Freshta and Laila walk home with their brother, recapping the game the entire way. The walk seems shorter going home than the thirty minutes it took to get there. They are coated in dust from the game. When the sisters reach their house, they have to heat buckets of water and wash thoroughly. That night they fall asleep easily, exhausted.

The second game is scheduled for the following Thursday. That morning, the Stars arrive at Hindu Kush Field only to learn that their opponents are none other than Hindu Kush, the home team.

Those girls are tall and strong. They have a crowd with them.

"What's happening?" Laila asks. In the first game, people along the sidelines were cheering the Stars. Now the chants are for Hindu Kush, and the Stars hear hostile slurs, teasing, attacks flung in their direction.

Uneasy, they do their warm-ups and then gather on the field. Samira pulls on her goalie gloves and trots back to goal. She is closest to the sidelines, a stationary target.

Laila can see how nervous she is, in the way she stares straight ahead, body still.

"They are all against us," Laila calls softly to Samira, who nods, grimly.

Laila decides not to stray far from the goal, to stay close.

Freshta dribbles the ball downfield, evading defenders, clearing a path to the goal. She has a clear shot, but at the last second she jerks the ball wide.

It rolls into the goalkeeper's hands.

Three times Freshta launches a drive the length of the field, outpacing opponents to earn an open shot. Three times she chokes.

"What are you doing?" Robina shouts. "Make the goal!"

"Robina *jan,* it's okay," Freshta answers, trying to calm her with a weak smile. Robina snaps her head back toward the ball.

From her position on defense, Laila watches in disbelief as her sister blows the shots.

She can't imagine what is happening. Each perfect pass she feeds to Freshta is being fumbled, inexplicably botched. Laila decides not to pass to her sister anymore.

She dribbles the ball upfield, as one of the boys calls out, "Shame on you—you used to play well, now you can't score!"

Flustered, Laila stumbles, and a Hindu Kush player swoops by and picks off the ball to cheers from the crowd.

. . .

The Stars warily eye the crowd. Everyone in the stands is against them.

Back on defense, Laila strips a Hindu Kush player of the ball and passes it back to Samira, to a clearing downfield. Samira leans forward to pick it up.

"Just kick it!" Robina yells at her.

Confused, Samira hesitates, caught between reaching out for the ball and trying to kick a pass to a nearby teammate. As she lifts her foot, the ball slides backward into her own net.

The crowd roars derisively: 1–0, Hindu Kush.

The referees blow the whistle for halftime.

The Stars walk to the sidelines, dazed. Their game has disintegrated. They stare at one another bleakly, filled with one another's mistakes, each bursting with everything that everyone else has done wrong. They are exhausted.

Kamran, Robina's coach from *Aschiana,* approaches them.

"Girls," he calls. "Come here."

They gather around him, shoulders slumped, embarrassed and angry.

"You are not passing the way you were before," he says, in a stern voice. "Each of you wants to make a goal by yourself!"

Robina, Laila, Miriam, and Freshta avoid looking at one another.

"You have to pass to each other to make goals."

He is right.

"The boys are saying things to me," Samira admits, her voice breaking.

Laila has an idea.

She goes up to Fawad and her brother, Abdullah, and quietly makes a request.

"Can you please keep the boys from yelling at us?"

As the second half starts, the Stars stride out on the field. Abdullah and Fawad take up positions behind Samira's net, arms folded, staring down the boys who have been taunting her. The chants haltingly subside.

On one pass upfield, Freshta scores. On another, it is Robina. Then Freshta again!

The Stars have suddenly pulled ahead, 3–1.

At the burst of scoring, their spirits rise.

The other team pressures the goal.

"Chick, get the ball!" Samira yells out to Laila, in English. At the phrase, Laila bursts into laughter. She doesn't run. She doubles over, staggering toward the ball, as Samira faces the girl bearing down on her. Samira knocks the shot away.

"Chick," she says mischievously to Laila. "That was not very helpful."

"Stop calling me that," Laila shoots back, giggling.

The Stars win 3–1, the only goal against them their own mistake.

"You girls are just flying in the air," Walizada tells them. He has a suspicion that they will win the tournament.

A ROUTINE EMERGES. Each night before the games, the Stars gather at Freshta and Laila's house. After the plates caked with rice and the empty *chay* cups have been cleared away, the girls gather in the sisters' room. They lock the door.

Then they crank up the cassette player and start to dance. Laila loves the exaggerated head and arm movements that go with Bollywood musicals. Robina dances to the twisting music of Shakira, pulling a scarf around her in a circle.

When they are tired, they settle on the floor for intense analysis sessions: what went wrong, what could be done better. They stay up late, strategizing, teasing, raking through every play.

"No matter what the goalkeeper does—just don't care, make the goal," Robina urges Freshta.

"Yes, Robina *jan*," Freshta says. Robina's unconvinced. Freshta *must* not be swayed by anything in the goalkeepers' eyes, even tears.

"*Eira baz na kaunid!*" she says fiercely. Next time, no more.

"It won't happen again!"

No issue is left unsaid. Nothing will fester. Every opinion, insight, critique is aired, and attacked, and resolved on the floor of the room.

At dawn, Robina pokes her teammates awake. It is time for *fajr*. Robina assembles the girls and together they recite the morning prayers.

"When it's seven o'clock, wake me again," Laila mumbles, turning over and sinking back into sleep.

"I don't want to make the *chay*," Freshta mumbles.

"*Chup bash*," Robina says, with a grin. Shut up.

They make the *chay,* along with breakfast, to the delight of the sisters' parents.

"Perhaps you'll wake up this early during the school year," Arzo suggests. There is no response.

The girls eat breakfast, then get ready for the game, stuffing uniforms into their bags, reminding each other of what needs to be done. By 7:30 A.M., they have left together and arrived at the field.

Miriam has never imagined anything like it.

life can be different

MIRIAM, KABUL AND AMERICA

"You become who you live with."
—AFGHAN SAYING

IRIAM WAS A child of war. Born just after the Soviets withdrew from Afghanistan, she was an infant when mujahideen warlords battled for control of Kabul, and a toddler when Kabul was bombed, and bombed again. By the time she turned six, more than 45,000 civilians had been killed in her city. Then the Taliban captured Kabul.

Growing up during the civil war, then the Taliban, Miriam knew that people died indiscriminately. It seemed sometimes as if lives were interchangeable. Friends, small children, and relatives were killed by bombings; people she knew and didn't know; strangers across the city, neighbors next door. She absorbed it, and went on.

Our people are in the streets and our people die for no rea-son because somebody else just puts a bomb there.

She'd walk through the streets of the Old City on her errands, without seeing, without feeling. It was the way things were: the rubble, houses with their windows smashed, streams of people in alleyways, children in rags, all so thin.

Now at fourteen, she is aware of a difference. She can cry.

Weaving through the narrow streets, she winces at the beggars, some with missing limbs, at the children standing with them, their palms held out, all day in the sun, baking and crisping like *naan*.

Our country is full of misery.

Everywhere, in the alleys and on the avenues, are weary men and boys standing behind their flat wooden carts, sell-ing something, anything. Police charge their small stands and beat them, yelling, "Clean up! Go away!"

They are only scraping together the small bits of money they can earn for their families.

Like my brothers.

The police chase them. Vendors get hurt. People are killed.

Like my father.

Now, traveling the streets of the Old City, she feels a deep-ening love in herself for her country, her people. She under-stands how much has been broken. Now there is something new inside herself—ambition.

Life can be different.

She knows this not only because of the families she met in America. They welcomed her and her teammates into their homes with traditional Afghan hospitality. She tries to carry this with her—to take care, offer the same trust, express the same kindness.

And she has felt the affection of strangers, the Afghan-American women crying and hugging each of her teammates, exclaiming, "Thank Allah that you can travel and come, and as a woman play soccer."

In America, thousands screamed encouragement when they played. It seemed to her that everyone she met urged her to play harder, to compete better, and excel in what she loved: playing soccer.

⚜

HER OLDER SISTER, Sahra, chides her: "How will soccer help you when you get married?" In the sandy cloister outside their two-room mud-brick house, Miriam roughly scrapes the dried rice off plates, hurrying so she can get to Freshta and Laila's house before the tournament.

"Nobody will ask, 'How well do you play soccer?' They will ask, 'How well do you do chores around the house?'" Sahra gives a short laugh. She hangs laundry on a line of rope strung between their home and their neighbor's.

Miriam quickly dips the plates into two wide bowls filled with water, then scrubs them off. Finishing, she grabs her bag and dashes down to the bus stop.

It is Wednesday, December 21. After the Stars' first win on Sunday, an easy 3–0 victory, they advanced to the second round of the five-game tournament. Their second game will be tomorrow.

Miriam joins her giddy teammates at Freshta and Laila's house.

Daud, one of Miriam's older brothers, works as a guard at their Roots of Peace practice field. The field is close to the sisters' home, and he stops by on his way home from work. He knocks on their door and asks to speak with Miriam.

Miriam appears.

"Aren't you coming home, Miriam *jan*?" he asks. "Why are you staying here?"

"We are all staying together before our game tomorrow," she explains. "I want to be with them."

Daud considers. The house has older men—the father, the brothers. Daud feels responsible for his sister. He wants Miriam to be safe, but he knows this family. They are respectable.

He agrees.

The girls spend the evening picking through photos, talking about their trip to America. They sing the choruses from their favorite American songs and laugh about the movie *Home Alone.*

They go over the advice of the coaches back in Connecticut, who broke down the game into small pieces, making each one easy to grasp: "Shoot with the top part of your foot, not your toe. Pass with the inside curve of your foot. Catch the ball with your forehead, shifting back just as it makes contact."

Details of their advice are dissected, each drill discussed. On the field in America, each part of the body was enlisted in mastering the ball. Off the field, the sessions of strategy taught them lessons—what happens away from the ball can matter most.

Each memory of their coaching is a reminder of their lack of direction, their lack of drills, their lack of practical instruction now. Because there was never a women's soccer program in Afghanistan, there are no trained women soccer coaches. Consequently, the girls have more experience than their coaches. Their complaints, however, are laced with pride. Now they teach themselves, strategize their own plays, running their own exercise regimen before the games.

Thursday morning, Robina wakes up first and brews *chay* for everyone. As the girls get up, they stuff their uniforms into their bags and pull on their flowing shirts, long pants, and *hijabs*. In the cold December air, they are glad for the covering.

By 7:30 A.M., they leave the house together. As they walk to the field, they repeat the advice they discussed the night before: Stay in position, don't swarm the ball, support on the pass. Before they know it, they arrive at Hindu Kush Field.

Miriam has never hoped for this, because it has been beyond her to imagine. She is with girls who love soccer as much as she does, who coordinate plans for the game and expect one another to execute them, who compete as a team on the field, and are friends after the game ends.

Being with them is one of the most important things that's happened to her.

MIRIAM WAS YOUNG when she first discovered soccer. Her two brothers would sometimes watch games on television and then hurry outside in the late afternoons to scrimmage with the neighbors.

Miriam would scramble up on the roof of their home and perch along the edge, peering down at the boys kicking and fumbling with the ball below. They were not very good. But Miriam was entranced.

She longed to join the games. When her brothers tramped back inside, complaining about aches in their feet or reliving plays from the afternoon, Miriam listened carefully.

It was dangerous to stay outside for too long. The country was in the middle of a civil war. Finally, Miriam, her three siblings, and their mother, Masuda, fled to her parents' village, Sham-i-lee, while their father, Kamran, stayed in Kabul.

A decade before, her mother and father had escaped from the village to Kabul, when their house was burned during the war against the Soviets.

After a month in Sham-i-lee, the fighting seemed to die down in Kabul, and Kamran sent word that they could return. The day they arrived, bombings began again.

"Why did you come back?" Kamran asked Masuda as the blasts rattled like earthquakes through the walls.

"You yourself asked us to come back!"

"I didn't know war would start again," he answered. "You must go back."

"No," Masuda said. "If you're living here, we will join you. We will not allow you to live here alone."

He tried to protest.

"If we're going, then you have to go with us," she said. "If you're staying here, we're staying with you."

"Okay," he said. "We'll stay in Kabul."

Kamran never seemed to be afraid of the rockets that screamed down daily into the city, shattering houses, streets, people. When they heard the firing, he would tell Masuda, "Take all the children and go to the underground rooms"—a network of dank, narrow caves dug out underneath the houses, like basements burrowed into the rocks.

"No," she would tell him. "I will stay with you. If we are going to die, we will die together. If we are going to live, we will live together."

Still, Masuda sent her children—Ahmad, Daud, Sahra, and Miriam—to safety underground, while she ran between her husband on the roof and her children, who stood in terror in the lightless, narrow rooms, unable to see.

When the Taliban arrived in 1996, promising stability and peace, Miriam and her family were hopeful. Here was a change from the forces that had mangled their city and murdered so many; here were Muslims who could bring peace to the country.

Then one day, her brothers, Ahmad and Daud, were rounded up during a soccer game and brought into the stadium. They returned nauseous and wouldn't speak of what they'd seen.

THAT THURSDAY, THE Stars win again, 3–1. Hoisting bags on their shoulders, they are getting ready to go back to Freshta and Laila's house, when Freshta's cell phone rings. She answers, then hands it to Miriam. It is Ahmad, her eldest brother.

"Your game is during the day, not at night," he argues.

Laila sees Miriam's expression.

"Stay," she says softly. "Come back with us."

Miriam turns off the phone.

"I don't have a choice," she says.

She waves good-bye to her teammates and heads back to her house. Perhaps this will appease Ahmad.

⸙

MIRIAM HAD ALWAYS loved Ahmad. When she was young, before he'd left for Iran to earn money for the family, they'd climb up to the roof, the sweep of the teeming city below. He was patient with her questions. He told her to have good friends and stay close with them; don't speak with strangers when you're bringing water to the house, and get home quickly.

Her other brother, Daud, younger than Ahmad, had been his opposite: always impatient and strict and quick to anger. When bathing, he demanded that Miriam and her sister prepare his clothes in advance. It meant arranging the towel, pressing the shirt and pants, gathering the socks—all neatly laid out and waiting. If they failed to move quickly enough, he cursed them.

If he wanted a glass of water, it had to be placed in front

of him instantly. Ahmad was always more patient. If Miriam and her sister prepared his clothes, he appreciated it; otherwise he would assemble his own outfits.

But then things changed.

It all started with the passing of their father, Kamran.

He loved his children, especially Miriam, his youngest child. When she was a toddler, he would come home from work and lift her into his lap, ruffle her hair, and speak to her in a soft voice. At night, she would cuddle next to him, his comforting arm around her as she slept.

He had driven a truck, then a taxi, but had left both pursuits because they were too dangerous, to sell kebobs from a stand on the side of the road.

One morning when Miriam was five, he woke at 4 A.M., clipped his nails, took a bath, and left, as usual. He'd always stay at his stand for hours, until the sun lowered and the streets cleared in the darkness, but this day, he returned home after just a few hours. He seemed nervous, as if he knew what was going to happen to him. His family felt it too. Miriam begged him not to go out again and smothered him with kisses. All the children pleaded with him to stay home and not go back to work. Miriam's mother, Masuda, joined them.

"Stay, just this once."

He kissed his wife on the cheek. "I promise I will stay home tomorrow."

That afternoon a car crashed into his stand. Daud, who was with him, managed to get his father to the hospital and stayed there all night. Family members had no way to reach one another. Afghanistan didn't yet have cell phone towers, and the fear of land mines kept landlines or telephone poles from being dug into the ground.

No one else in the family knew what had happened— only that neither Daud nor Kamran came home that night. Miriam's uncles, cousins, and brothers scoured the city streets until three in the morning, but they couldn't find them. The next morning, Kamran passed away at the hospital and his body was brought back to the house.

Miriam couldn't stop weeping. When visitors came to the house, she clung to them, begging, "Take me. Take me with you."

"What are you saying?" cried Masuda.

"My father's not here with us so I don't want to stay here!"

She moved in with her grandmother, just down the hill. Despite daily visits and entreaties from her mother and brothers, she would not return. She believed that if she waited, her father would come home.

"You have to come and live with us, with your mother, with your brothers, with your own family," they told her. "Come back home."

Five months later, as Masuda made another entreaty, Miriam finally believed them. She leaned forward and kissed Masuda.

"You are my mother and father now," she said. "You mean both to me."

.   .   .

Ahmad and Daud were just beginning school when their father was killed. In that moment, they were no longer just sons. At twelve and ten, they became the heads of the family.

They had to leave school and work on the streets to support their family. They sold incense on makeshift stands and fruit out of wooden carts; they fixed car parts in mechanic shops. They never returned to school or learned to read or write. Miriam, then five, was forced to leave school the following year when the Taliban arrived.

Food became scarce. From three meals a day, now they were down to eating only one.

Nine years passed. Daud knew his life would never be more than it already was. Unable to read, he would never be able to pursue a career or have any choices. But when the Taliban left Kabul in 2001, the schools opened again. Miriam had a chance to re-enroll.

Ahmad protested sending her to school. Daud argued with him.

"She must not become like us. Miriam's future can be better."

He thought to himself: *It must be.*

Ahmad's objections were supported by an array of aunts, uncles, cousins: *What was the point? And to what end? To get a job? What will people say if she works? That our family cannot support her?*

The family's disapproval weighed heavily on Ahmad. As the eldest, he heard from them at every gathering, at the bazaar, when they came to his cart, their comments falling like droppings around his stall. He knew that in their homes, out of his earshot, they would say that his family was not a good one, that Miriam was a *batar-bya,* defiant, daughter.

Masuda ended the argument.

"My daughter must be educated," she said. "She must have a future."

When their mother joined in, Ahmad relented.

Miriam enjoyed school. Soon, she also enrolled in *Aschiana.* Some girls in the neighborhood had joined, and Masuda learned that their families were receiving rations. She brought her daughter to the nearest center, in De Afghanan.

At first, neither place offered chairs and tables to students. They did lessons sitting on the ground, pressing paper against walls, the backs of books, or on the floor. But school offered more subjects—like geography, social science, and Islamic studies—and Miriam's classmates were friendlier.

At *Aschiana,* alliances among students shifted quickly.

When she studied for a test at school, friends would lend their notes to help her prepare. At *Aschiana,* no one would lend her even a pencil.

Miriam knew that the students were very poor; many collected paper on the streets or sold water during the day. They had very little and clung to the possessions they'd accrued over the years. She knew this. But it still hurt.

Then *Aschiana* gained an undeniable edge. One day, a gym teacher entered Miriam's class.

"We are starting a soccer team," she announced. "Whoever is interested can join."

Immediately, Miriam flung up her hand.

. . .

She had never played or practiced before, but she trembled at the thought of finally being able to learn. When she stepped out onto the dirt pitch, though, her teammates seemed more committed to fighting than competing.

They shouted at each other to pass the ball, and when it didn't come to them, they would yell.

"Why didn't you pass it to me?"

Like Miriam, they had no skills or training. Few had even seen soccer before. The teacher seemed just as confused, content to let the girls kick the ball around on the dusty ground. Miriam learned to scrap for herself on the field.

Then a man arrived at *Aschiana*, an American. Miriam learned that he was selecting students to train in a special soccer program—he would be conducting interviews that afternoon.

She sat in the classroom filled with other girls waiting to be interviewed.

Miriam looked around.

All the other girls are so much older.

She felt younger, smaller.

They will probably be the ones who will be selected for the program. Not me.

Then the teacher had announced the results. Two girls had been accepted: Miriam and a girl she didn't know, Samira.

Stunned, Miriam locked eyes with Samira. They grinned at each other.

There were eight girls in total selected for the new team. They practiced at a place called the Afghan Center every week, where they also took English and computer lessons.

At *Aschiana,* they played on packed dirt that turned quickly to mud. The floors were dusty cement, and the winds whipped dust into their eyes, all over their clothes.

At the Afghan Center, the floors were tiled and swept clean every day. Outside, the girls ran across a simple yard, bounded by walls.

Miriam's teammates were generous. They learned together, studied together, practiced together, and loved one another.

When it was confirmed that Miriam had been selected for the American trip, she went home and told her family.

"They're taking us to America so we can study," she said carefully. "We will learn English there."

Masuda and Daud supported this chance for Miriam to continue her studies and it was quickly agreed: She would go. Daud would take the heat for the decision when telling Ahmad, who was now living in Iran.

The night before the team left for America, Miriam packed her bag for the six weeks: two pairs of jeans, two shirts, a pair of shoes; a toothbrush, toothpaste, and a hairbrush. She tucked away cookies from one of her aunts, raisins and chickpeas from Daud, and boiled eggs from another aunt.

She also put in pictures of her family—her father, mother, brothers, sister, uncles, aunts, cousins.

Then she went over to her mother.

"I'm afraid," she said.

One of their relatives had worked on a cargo plane. It crashed, killing him.

"What if my plane crashes?"

"It won't crash," Masuda said.

She pulled back and met Miriam's eyes.

"But you have to make sure you are not too afraid," she said. "This is your own decision to go and you have to be strong enough for it."

I have to be strong.

That night they slept beside each other. Miriam knew she wouldn't see her mother again for a long time.

The plane was just as terrifying as she'd imagined. It was so large—how could it possibly lift into the air? She sat next to Nadia, and they clutched each other throughout the flight, shrieking when the plane rocked up and down. Hours later, they landed in America.

Despite their informal practices in Afghanistan, the girls were still beginners. Someone would throw the ball down and everyone would run after it.

"You should not all run after the ball," their coach, Ali, instructed them.

Miriam listened soberly.

A few days later, they competed in their first game, at the Afghan-American Soccer Cup in Virginia. Miriam frowned as a whole group of her teammates clamored after the ball in a large cluster of bodies.

She hurried off the field to tell Ali.

"You're not supposed to get off the field!" he called as he saw her trotting toward him. "Just go and play!"

"But you said we shouldn't all run after the ball," she explained.

"You're not supposed to do this either!"

Miriam ran back onto the field and tried to separate herself from her teammates.

"Get scattered!" she yelled at them. "Don't all run after the ball!"

She stood by herself, to the side of the field.

"I'm open!" she called. But no one passed to her.

Still, the game was a draw, and afterward each of them received medals. It was Miriam's first.

Off the field, some of her teammates could be prickly. Once during practice she took a sip from Freshta's water bottle.

"Why did you drink from my water?" Freshta shouted.

Miriam put the water bottle down.

"Forgive me," she said softly after a moment. "You can use my stuff if you want."

Freshta looked like she wanted to say more, but when Miriam didn't argue further, she calmed down. "Okay," she said.

Freshta was brave; she knew how to swim and would propel herself into the deep end of the pool at Barbara and Duaine's house.

"Join me!" she called to the other girls, but they didn't know how to swim.

At first, Miriam would only wade into the water up to her knees. But when she saw the other girls splashing around, she felt encouraged.

Soon, she was plunging her head underwater and shaking the water off in sprays of shimmering drops.

. . .

Through her new friends, Miriam became braver. Their first week, the girls went to an Afghan-American dentist, Dr. Riaz Rayek. As Dr. Rayek approached her gently with a needle, Miriam twisted away.

"You went through the Taliban and conquered them," he teased. "That's much tougher than fixing a few teeth. So why are you afraid?"

That may have been true. But when Miriam saw him approaching her mouth with sharp silver instruments, she couldn't have cared less about the Taliban.

Dr. Rayek brought her in to watch Samira have her teeth drilled, to show that it didn't hurt. Miriam entered the room suspiciously. She eyed Samira, her small body reclining on the chair.

Samira smiled at her. All the time the doctor hovered over her mouth, she didn't make a sound.

When it was Miriam's turn, she squeezed her eyes shut.

"How many teeth did you fill?" she asked when he announced he'd finished.

"You didn't notice?" he asked, smiling. "Two."

A few days later, Nadia, Robina, and Miriam were home alone; the other girls had gone for follow-up work with Dr. Rayek.

Left alone, the girls quickly gathered at the pool. Nadia, who knew how to swim, motioned Miriam forward, intending to hold her steady—but Miriam's foot slipped. She slid down the slick incline into the deep end.

She screamed and then sunk under the water. Nadia and Robina frantically tried to grab her hair, her shirt, anything, and pull her to the surface, but Miriam's frenzied kicking dragged them down under the water too.

Finally, Robina scrambled to the side of the pool. Grabbing onto the edge, she extended her other arm outward and reached Miriam's arm. She pulled her to the corner and hauled her onto the ground. Miriam coughed up water and nearly fainted.

Shaken, the three girls lay quietly on the solid ground until the rest of the group returned home.

Miriam was wary of water after that. But when the team visited the beach, she was fascinated. The sky-colored sea stretched out, clear and seemingly endless. Fishermen stood along a bridge, casting nets that caught up clattering bundles of lobsters and crabs.

Samira forged ahead into the waves. Miriam rolled up her pants to her knees. She and Nadia held hands and stepped forward. They rushed in until the shock of water doused their toes, then they ran back, grabbing sand and throwing it at each other, giggling.

"If either of us loses control," they told each other, "then we will pull the person out and save them."

All day, they didn't let go.

Miriam knew she had only been allowed to go to America because she had claimed the trip was for education. Soccer would have been pushing too far. Ahmad was in Iran at the time, and her mother and Daud were glad to see her seizing opportunities and gaining new experiences. They had not questioned her too closely.

When Miriam admitted the real nature of the American trip—over the phone, from Connecticut—Ahmad was enraged. He would never have let her go if he had known. Daud kept his thoughts to himself.

15

winning

MIRIAM, KABUL, DECEMBER 2005

"The deeper that sorrow carves into your being, the more joy you can contain."
—KAHLIL GIBRAN

 T THEIR HINDU Kush tournament, the Stars continue to win, defeating their third team, 2–0. The next game, on the following Monday, will decide whether the Stars advance to the championship.

That Monday, Miriam wakes up at 7 A.M. and prepares for the semifinal game. She assembles her uniform—the blue warm-up suit with a black slash across the front, her tan visor with the interlocking N and Y sewn across the front, her soccer cleats—and packs them into her satchel. She pulls her hair into a neat bun and covers it by tugging at her scarf. She must meet the Roots of Peace car at 10 A.M. and she wants to be ready. Her mother and sister are also about to leave, for a family gathering.

"Are you coming?" her mother asks, assuming she'd go with them.

"No, *madar jan,* I have a game."

Ahmad is listening.

"If you don't go with your mother," he says carefully, "then you're not allowed to go to soccer either."

"What do you mean?"

Miriam starts to tremble.

"What's the need for girls to play soccer?" he asks. Then, "There's no need."

Tears burn behind her eyes.

"I *want* to play," she says. "We are competing in a tournament, my team needs me."

"It's enough that you're going to school," he says, as she starts to cry. "That's all for you."

Between sobs, she argues, "But if I play I will be strong, and fit, and live longer. I must play, I love it!" She calls to her mother, crying, "*Madar, madar.*"

"Whatever your brother says, you have to accept," Masuda says, and turns to leave.

Miriam understands—her mother has drawn a line about what she will fight for, what she will challenge, and soccer and school are on opposite sides.

"*None* of our relatives play," Ahmad says. "Why should you?"

He will not be persuaded, Miriam can see that. She starts for the door, to head for the field.

"If you go outside," he shouts, "I'll break your legs."

Miriam knows he is just trying to scare her. But she

also knows that he does not intend to let her play, ever again.

She sits down on the carpeted floor of their house and weeps. She cries for more than an hour, past the time when she is to meet the Roots of Peace car across town.

When Daud returns home on his lunch break, he is surprised to see her still there. He notes her packed bag and her street clothes—the long, baggy shirt just above her knees, over loose pants.

"Don't you have a game?" he asks.

She looks up bleary-eyed and explains.

"I allow you to go," he says.

Miriam scrambles to her feet. Daud motions her through the door; it is okay, he has given permission. He will answer for it.

She grabs her bag and runs out the door. Daud follows. Ahmad, standing outside the house, sees his sister, clutching her soccer bag. He is astonished.

"It's okay, let her go," Daud says, coming out behind her. "They're going to find out if they're the top team or not," he explains. "We should let her go and play and see if they win."

Miriam waits as the brothers argue in the rocky cloister outside their home, waving their arms, negotiating over the end of her soccer career.

"Let her go for this last round," Daud says finally. "When she finishes this tournament, these two games, then after that, that's all."

Miriam accepts this compromise for now, focused on

today's game, on catching the car, which may already have left. She races down the steep, rocky path to the road, where she hops on a bus to the Roots of Peace office. When she arrives, the girls are gone.

Their coach Fawad, though, is still there, putting his last things together. Miriam runs up to his car and jumps in.

Miriam and Fawad arrive at Hindu Kush Field. Her teammates—Laila, Freshta, Samira, Robina—are out on the grounds, a brown, dusty stretch of rubble-strewn land marked by thin white goalposts. Blue-shadowed mountains rise in the distance, blending into the sky. Ridges of snow seem to float in the cold winter air.

Miriam drops her bag, tears off her shoes, and slips into her cleats. She pulls off her scarf, shoves on her visor, and runs out onto the field.

She rushes to meet her teammates: Freshta and Laila, their billowing ponytails spilling out over the backs of their visors, black waves against their dark blue warm-up suits; the slim, sturdy figure of Samira, her hair neatly tucked underneath a faded black visor; and Robina, with her visor twisted backward like a tan bandage across her forehead.

At Miriam's approach, the girls smile, then turn toward the other team. Freshta shakes her head. It doesn't look good. The other team is bigger, stronger. The girls exchange worried glances.

Further complicating things are the Stars' newest players. To this point, they have played five against six in every game. But the team was told by the tournament organizers that a full roster was needed for the final two games.

The Stars scrambled to find friends to join them as additional players on the team. They turned up four—Zainafshan, Lailee, Benazir, and Nazia—but these girls had limited experience with soccer. In fact, these were their first real games. They stand awkwardly on the field, excited, but unsure what to do.

As the game starts, Miriam blocks out thoughts of her brothers, their "agreement," and what it will mean. She tries to focus on the ball. *Forget everything and focus.*

The ball soars toward her. She kicks. Her thoughts are tethered to the arc of the ball. It lands.

The girls from the other team seem to have a density that makes them solid, but they're also slower than the younger and slighter Stars. At each Star steal or slick pass, the small audience along the sandy sidelines—mainly other teams from the tournament—erupts into cheers.

The Stars sprint, kicking up clouds of dust. Dust smears across their faces, covers their hair, makes them cough. The cold wind is drawn into their lungs with each gulp of icy breath. Still they run.

They run because that is their only advantage. The Stars easily streak around the other team. They snatch passes and push ahead, with small, quick bursts of speed. Miriam darts in and out, getting behind the other team, skimming the ball from their feet. Freshta and Robina reel in the passes and dribble ferociously up the field.

But their opponents block the shots. And their kicks are stronger—when they gain control of the ball, they barrel forward.

A goal by Freshta breaks the stalemate. The Stars escape with a narrow 1–0 victory.

Miriam enters her house. She is beaming.

"We are in the championship game! We won!"

Ahmad shrugs.

"What's it to me that you won?" he asks. "There's no benefit to me whether you won or you lost."

"It's no concern to you," Miriam replies, "but to *me*. I'm a good player."

The Stars have made it to the finals.

⁊⁊⁊

THE CHAMPIONSHIP WILL be held in Ghazi Stadium. Since its construction in 1923, it has remained the country's national stadium. The area surrounding it is empty, dust-colored land, where boys sometimes gather to play pickup soccer. It's flanked by wide, well-paved roads that host national parades. The stadium appears almost incongruous on the flat landscape.

Huge, battered metal gates swing onto a large open ground surrounded by immense concrete walls. During the years of the Taliban, Miriam's brothers were once herded into the stadium to watch an execution, before stumbling back to the house, sick. Today, on December 28, 2005, the same stadium will be hosting a girls' soccer championship.

That morning, a Wednesday, Miriam packs her uniform and cleats in her sports bag.

"I am going to Ghazi Stadium today, to play for the championship," she announces to her family.

Her mother, sister, and two brothers are silent. This will be her last game. Whether the Stars win or lose, it will be her last. Still, no one says a word.

But Miriam is excited. She wants to win. She wants to be first and not second to anyone else. Yes, Ahmad is upset. But right now Miriam cares only about winning.

At Freshta and Laila's house, the rest of the girls wake up early. They are too excited to eat. They hurriedly brew *chay* for the family and then pile into the waiting Roots of Peace car. As they are driven to the stadium, they realize they are starving.

The car pulls up to the stadium. The other team hasn't arrived, which is not surprising—the Stars are more than an hour early. Even though Miriam didn't spend the night, she has managed to meet them at the field. The team looks around and gawks.

The gates are flung open. A flash of green. They walk onto a vast grass field, ringed by rows and rows of rising concrete seats. Towering over them are giant posters of the men governing Afghanistan's recent past and present: the King, Ahmad Shah Baba; the Lion, Massoud; the President, Karzai.

Laila speaks for all of them, "Are we really playing here?"

The girls stare at one another. It is enormous.

"Thanks to Allah we are playing in this field," Laila says fervently. "And not the dusty one."

Nearby two boys are selling *bolani*—flattened fried dough filled with potatoes and leeks. Laila eagerly buys two.

"Don't eat a lot," Fawad warns, but she needs to eat something.

Laila approaches Robina—"Take some," she says. Robina breaks off a small piece.

"You didn't have breakfast," Laila scolds her gently. Robina never eats much before a game. Laila urges her to take a few more bites.

The Stars run their own warm-up. They race the length of the field, forward and back. In spite of the cold, they lower themselves onto the frigid ground, stretching their legs, placing the soles of their feet together, loosening up their bodies. They leap to their feet and perform jumping jacks, or, as they call them, jumping stars.

They pass and kick a ball back and forth. Samira shouts, "Shoot to me," as she moves to the goal, to practice blocking shots.

They should ignore the other team. But furtive glimpses reveal strong, crisp kicks. They are considered the top team in the tournament. The Stars are acutely aware of their own thin arms, skinny legs, slight frames. The oldest among them, Freshta, is fifteen. Most are fourteen.

The referee blows the whistle. The game begins. The American-trained players rush through every position, getting little help from their new teammates. They run frantically across the field. On defense, Laila sprints forward up the field to make sure the ball clears. Freshta, on offense, hustles back to protect the goal when the other team steals possession.

The vastness of the field is no longer inspiring—it is end-less. They run and run and run.

The other team's leader, Soraya, is strong and fierce. As Freshta pushes the ball up the field, Soraya cuts over and strikes at the ball. Her foot smacks into Freshta's knee. Soraya trips and sprawls on the ground and Freshta loses her foot-ing. She skids forward, slamming her knee down.

The referee hurries over. "Are you hurt? Do you need to sit this out?"

Freshta waves him off. Both girls scramble to their feet.

But when Robina dashes in front of the goal and Freshta tries to shoot her a pass, Freshta feels a pain and warmth around her knee. She looks down. There is blood.

At 5,900 feet above sea level, the city is close to the sky. In the thin Kabul air, all the girls gasp for breath. The sun is beating down from directly overhead; it is nearly midday. Freshta cannot keep playing. She stumbles over to the bench and grabs her water bottle. Wiping sweat from her eyes, she leans against the bench and drinks deeply. She is almost ready to give up.

Fawad is shouting at them, "Run!" "Defend!" "Get back!" The new players are hovering on the field, yelling back, "What should I do? What should I do now?"

The other team presses toward the Stars goal.

The new players freeze. "Should we take the ball?" Nasima shouts in panic.

"Kick the ball!" Freshta screams. "Just kick the ball!"

Other teams from the tournament, along with their coaches, Olympic officials, people working in the stadium, and embassy representatives, sit on the concrete tiers. During the men's final team practice, the Olympic officials announced the girls' game, and the male soccer players fill out the lower rows of the stands.

The crowd cheers on the Stars; cameramen keep pace on the sidelines as they play.

And then it ends. No one has scored during regulation.

Penalty kicks.

Each team selects four players, who will alternate shots on the goal. The team with the most goals scored will be the champions. No other players are allowed on the field, except the shooter and the goalie, tensed in the suddenly cavernous space between the goalposts.

The referee places the ball on the field for the first shot.

Freshta steps forward, her knee throbbing. She hears taunting behind her, predicting her shot will fly over the goal. It does. 0–0.

Robina's shot is also out. 0–0.

Laila rears back and launches a hard shot past the goalkeeper's lunging arms—but it smacks against the bar and rebounds out. 0–0.

Each team alternates taking penalty shots on the goalie.

Samira has caught or deflected every opposition shot near the goal. She leans forward, flexing her hands, arms slightly raised, a crease of concentration between her eyes.

Lailee, who started playing soccer just a few weeks before, steps up to the ball. She is the final kicker of the day.

"Aim for the corner," Laila advises her.

Lailee runs at the ball and blasts it with her toe. It speeds across the grass—right through the goalkeeper's legs. The Stars have won! They are the *qahraman*. Champions.

The Stars pour onto the field, screaming. They throw their arms around one another, hugging and jumping in the center of the field. They break apart, clapping, laughing, racing around the field, arms in the air. They are quickly surrounded by reporters and coaches and players from other teams. Everyone congratulates the champions of the first Afghan women's soccer tournament.

Journalists search for girls to interview. Freshta, elected their captain two weeks before, steps forward. She joins captains from two other teams in an interview, broadcast over the radio. Freshta explains that she and her teammates trained in the States.

"When you went to America, did you become an American?" asks the announcer.

"No."

"How are the people there?"

"Much better than the people in Afghanistan," she says cheekily. She smiles. "They are very friendly."

The interviewer has another question: "Lots of Afghans believe that girls shouldn't be playing soccer—they ask, 'Why are they playing?'"

"Before the Taliban, women were playing sports," Freshta asserts.

A woman calls the radio studio. She agrees with Freshta's points, but with some caveats.

"If you go to America and want to play soccer, you have to wear a head scarf," she instructs.

A man calls in to respond.

"Before these wars, women weren't wearing scarves," he argues. "They were playing sports and no one could tell them what to do."

After the interview is over, the reporter looks at Freshta— slight, long, wild black hair, her eyes slightly wide at what she has just done.

"You were very brave," he tells her. "I've never seen a person talk like you!"

Afghan Football Federation officials approach various team members. One strides across the field and takes four girls aside: Robina, Laila, Freshta, and Samira. Miriam stands by herself. She doesn't go over to them. Her teammates are beaming and nodding as the official talks to them. Miriam waits for him to come to talk to her, but he doesn't. It dawns on her. She is the only American-trained Star not selected for the national team. Not that she would have been able to play anyway.

She tries to hold onto her happiness; it almost escapes her, like a small bird in her hand. She thinks to herself, *We have defeated the strongest team. We won.*

We are the top team among all the teams that exist.

The next day, the Stars return to Ghazi Stadium, where they each receive a medal and the team gets one trophy— this time for winning. After the ceremony, the girls take a Roots of Peace car back to the office. They roll down the windows and dangle the trophy outside as they shriek with laughter.

Daud is waiting for Miriam. He proudly shouts at the sight of the trophy. The girls get out of the car and he shakes their hands in congratulation. For Miriam, he opens his arms wide and wraps her in a huge hug.

"Congratulations," he whispers.

Miriam presents her medal that night to her mother—a golden circle suspended from a red and white ribbon. Her mother holds it in her hand and smiles.

Miriam takes back the medal. She walks over to Ahmad, to show him. He looks surprised.

"How did my sister play so well?" he asks, impressed in spite of himself. "I didn't think you could win."

"I told you so many times that I'm a good player," she says. "But you never listen."

Later that night, the euphoria of winning fades. She has played her last game. Now it is over.

She takes her medal off, and slowly puts it away.

flying away

AUGUST 2004

AILA. FRESHTA. SAMIRA. Miriam. Deena. Nadia. Ariana. Robina. When they arrived in America, little did I know that I'd not only find some part of my other half, but that in fact I'd be plunked down in the middle of its culture, mores, and language.

I was embarrassed that I'd lost so much of my mother tongue. At night while the girls were asleep, I'd be doing the accounts, sitting in the laundry room as their T-shirts, shorts, socks, and other clothes spun around in the washer. I'd wonder: *What am I? Am I Afghan? Afghan-American? American? A combination of them all?*

Here were these girls, straight from Afghanistan, experiencing an all-embracing, but completely different society. Yet their culture, their religion, their language were so deeply embedded in them, they didn't have to think about it.

Likewise American culture and English were embedded in me. But these six weeks turned me toward Afghanistan: I was speaking more Pashto. I was beginning to learn Dari.

Then, in the moment when the girls greeted my parents one final time before leaving, I realized what I had done: I'd brought Afghanistan to me.

⁂

WE WERE AT the JFK airport, checking in the mounds of luggage.

"You have to come to Kabul, Awista *jan*," the girls pleaded, circling around me.

"Don't worry, I'm coming." I did not want to cry. "I'll be there soon. I'll see you girls again."

I watched them walk toward the checkpoint, heavy with their sports bags slung over their shoulders. When they got through the gate, I started to sob.

The girls turned in one seamless move, together, and waved good-bye.

I waved back. "I'll see you," I whispered. "I promise."

I thought of the medals they were taking home, and wondered what exactly it was they had won, and what part of it they might be able to keep. What would happen to them now in Afghanistan I could only imagine.

Some of it I could not imagine at all.

the journey home

KABUL, APRIL 2006

"Marg-e nedaragem khalko
Ka de watan pa hadeeroke khawre shoma."

"Take me once to my own home
In a strange earth one's dignity is decreased."
—FARHAD DARYA, AFGHAN SINGER

LYING TOWARD DUBAI, on my way to Afghanistan, I felt I was shedding one life, in the States, floating in an in-between space, ready to descend into another life. As we circled toward the runway, my heart raced, my mind looped around and around: *Turn back right now, fly home. Home? I am going* toward *home.*

We finally landed. I walked into the huge, glass-domed Dubai terminal and headed straight for the marble restroom.

My transformation would began here. After I changed out of my jeans and T-shirt, I stared at my image in the mirror; a red veil covered my hair and my shoulders, a white tunic fell to my knees.

Two hours later, the Ariana Afghan flight lifted off from Dubai. The uneasiness I'd felt lifted along with the plane. There was no going back.

Soon I would touch the soil of my homeland. I would see the sign, "Welcome to Kabul," see the girls again. I was ready for the moment, yet afraid of what I'd find.

"You do not know how hard it is,

. . . emerging from one's secret dream
to voicing the dream."
—LAILA AL-SA'IH

"*Salaam,* Awista." A tall, solid man greeted me with a great smile. It was my driver, Zia, holding a piece of cardboard with my name printed on it.

"*Alaykom assalam,*" I responded and settled in the backseat of his white Toyota Corolla. The air was crisp and cool, the sky a bright blue. Even from inside the car, the sunlight was blinding, shimmering on the mountains like a silver sheet.

I squinted through the window as we made our way into Kabul. Groups of schoolgirls wove though the streets like grounded flocks of birds in their black uniforms and white head scarves; customers loaded strips of fresh, brown flat bread into bags; piles of pomegranates, watermelons, oranges, and dates shone in mounds of startling color; women with head scarves of palest blue or deep red milled before shops; armored military trucks honked and barreled their way through the traffic.

"So many beautiful colors," I whispered.

We continued down Airport Boulevard, past billboards and stalls, past bombed buildings and new, partially built towers. Earth-colored homes were crammed along the mountainsides, their doors painted in intense blues, greens, and reds. The streets of Kabul were a maze, ancient and intricate to the extreme.

"Lots of people," Zia said, and laughed, turning around in his seat. I was lucky. With many meetings and a tight schedule, I would have Zia for my guide, my "sometimes" interpreter, and my driver.

The girls were a series of vivid pictures in my mind. But two years is a long time. Now I was here, in Kabul, in their country, and mine. I wanted to see them. Would they remember me? If so, how?

I'd be in Kabul for more than a month. But I'd given myself a lot to do: first, to see the girls again. I'd phoned some and sent messages to the others. Then, I'd scheduled interviews with sports officials, in order to get an idea of where sports were headed in the country. I was organizing a weeklong girls' soccer clinic in conjunction with the Afghanistan Football Federation. To help run the clinic, four Afghan-American soccer coaches were set to arrive from the States, and I was responsible for all logistics for the program. We'd also be assisting the federation with their girls' soccer tournament.

A week later, the four coaches and I traveled by car to the *quloop askari,* military field, located near Massoud Circle, one of the busiest intersections in Kabul. We drove through the high security gate into the flat, grassy pitch. Despite the noise just beyond the walls, the field inside was vast and quiet.

There, in red uniforms of loose-fitting pants and long-sleeved shirts, were Samira, Robina, Ariana, Laila, and Freshta, kicking a white ribbed soccer ball to one another. The five girls looked up as our team of coaches arrived. They turned toward us, the sun behind them. It was as if they were lit from within, on fire.

Robina waved and yelled, "*Salaam,* Awista *jan!*"

One by one I hugged and kissed the girls. When I first met them at Barbara Goodno's home in Maryland, they looked so young. Now they looked older, more mature, and while they had lost some of the youthful features to their faces, these were now replaced by older, more mature souls. I recognized them, and emotions flooded my mind as I remembered each one of them and their unique experience in the States. I would now be able to forge new memories of them, and this time in the place we both call home.

❦

THE FIVE GIRLS had been playing soccer every Friday. Their practice expanded when we set up the clinic, and they became coach's assistants, helping to train the younger and newer girls. One afternoon, after a long, arduous practice, Robina asked if I could give her a ride home.

We arrived at the base of the rugged hill where Robina lived. From afar, the sight of homes built into the mountains was breathtaking, but up close, it was harsh—homes without sewage systems, running water, even windowpanes.

We left the panting Toyota at the bottom of a sheer, narrow path and began hiking up the hill. Zia would pick me up here later. Along the mountainside were graves, marked by jagged splinters of stone and uneven spikes hammered into the ground.

Robina led the way, lithe as a gazelle. I gasped and tried to catch my breath. It wasn't far, but it was steep, and Kabul was already one of the highest capitals in the world.

"I can barely breathe," I wheezed.

We continued our ascent. Above me, Robina waved cheerily. Pausing briefly, I looked around. All below me was the dusty, sun-drenched landscape of Kabul. I was in *Afghanistan*. I felt a sudden jolt, as if I had just been transported here, a magic sleight of hand, a shearing of distance and time.

Ten minutes later, we reached Robina's house.

Her home was set back from a wall and gate, perched on a shelf of rock. The family had been hacking into the side of the mountain to clear more land; the remnants of blocks of limestone were scattered about. I scrambled up stacked rocks to reach the door.

Robina offered to take my bag. "*Khosh amaded*," she said as we stepped inside. Welcome.

The front room was cozy and delicate. Simple lace curtains hung over each of the two doorways. On the windowsill, a pair of white doves cooed in a cage. Outside, the *Azan*, the ancient call for prayer, echoed over the city.

Robina ducked behind a curtain and returned carrying a

teapot and plates of small, sweet cookies, which she placed on the table.

We spoke of her family and mine. She had questions about my visit, and I had questions about her schooling. I looked around the room. Her soccer awards were on a table by themselves, polished and shining.

"So, Robina *jan,* tell me, what do your neighbors and friends think of your soccer accomplishments?"

"The neighbors are not as good as they should be," she said. "They are jealous people. I don't share my soccer with them. After your visit, they will ask me, 'Why does she come to your house? What does she give you?'" She shook her head.

So there it was. It was about being an outsider. One of "those people." Robina averted her eyes. A typical politeness here, so as not to see someone's hurt or embarrassment.

The neighbors' reactions didn't surprise me. I knew how our community could come to quick, harsh judgments. On the other hand, there were plenty of "those people" to gripe about. For decades in Afghanistan, a seemingly never-ending procession of foreigners had decided the country's fate.

But I was Afghan. *Wasn't I?*

"Why didn't you tell me it's a problem to visit?" I asked softly.

"I wanted you to come."

I changed the subject. "How are practices going?"

Now Robina sparkled. "We play better and better. Now everyone respects me at school because I play soccer— because I play soccer very well."

She rushed out of the room and returned with a medal

she'd received at Kabul's most recent female soccer tournament.

"Beautiful," I said. And I meant it. Not the medal, but her, her face flushed with pride. *This* was what I had come to see.

We were at ease with each other now. I felt I could ask. "Robina *jan,* what is life like here now?"

"Who knows if we go out today and some blast happens? Even when we go to school, we are very afraid. If a crowd gathers in a place, we run from there because we are afraid of suicide bombings in crowded places."

My heart lurched.

I held her hand. "You are very brave, Robina *jan.*"

COMING HOME TO Afghanistan was not what I'd imagined.

On the one hand, on the streets all the faces seemed familiar, a vast ocean of mirrored images. I could see my mother's, my father's, my own. The feeling was akin to seeing someone whom you knew as a child, unformed and fresh, and then meeting her as an adult, her face marked, the voice deeper and richer than you remembered. To find myself in the majority was strange and wonderful too, unlike how I felt in the States. And hearing Dari and Pashto everywhere immersed me in it as if I were underwater. But too there were moments when I felt I was drowning.

One evening, the four coaches and I decided to have dinner at the Serena Hotel, located in the center of Kabul. I invited Zia and his cousin, Samim, to join us.

The hotel was extravagant by any measure: fountains, marble floors, huge bouquets of flowers, with thick, red-hued Afghan carpets layering the walls. In the dining room a large buffet was laid out in gorgeous piles. We got our dishes and sat down at our round table covered in white linen, damask napkins, and a centerpiece of miniature pink roses. The food was delicious.

Then the bill came. There were seven of us, and the coaches and I were treating Zia and his cousin. The tally was around $250 American. While we dug in our bags and wallets, Zia glanced at the total and sighed softly.

The next morning, as we were preparing to leave, he told me, "I couldn't sleep last night."

"Why, Zia?"

"I was thinking about the bill."

"The bill?" Did he mean his own payment for his work?

"Last night. It was a shock to see the cost of one dinner. I could feed my family for a long time on that."

A mistake. "American" generosity. An "American" lack of understanding, or awareness. Two hundred and fifty dollars is what most Afghans make in a year.

At that moment I understood "the bifurcation of exile." The hyphenated person. Not exactly a blend; not exactly Afghan, not exactly American. In America, I had grown up in Afghan culture, knew its mores and ways, and yet here in Kabul was a bridge I couldn't seem to cross.

One day a woman at the market stopped me. "You've not

been living here all your life, am I right?" She could tell from the way I wore my *hijab,* covering my head and shoulders but not wrapped around my upper body in the manner most local women wore it.

Another afternoon, I visited Freshta and Laila's home. When I got there, I absentmindedly invited Zia into the house.

When we entered the large front room, Duaine was already seated. I knew from our continued correspondence that he'd stayed close with the sisters' family, so it was no surprise to see him there. *Chay* steaming and hot and sweet cookies laid out on the tray were set delicately on a low, round carved table before him.

I greeted Duaine, and Zia and I sat down. Duaine poured tea, and we chatted awhile. Then I noticed: No women other than myself were present. I looked at Duaine, a question in my eye.

"An unfamiliar man in their home," he said, meaning Zia. "One they don't know. The women are in the other room."

Of course!

Blushing, I rose and went to the back room. Freshta and Laila got up from the mat. "Awista *jan,* we are so happy you are here." I was hugged, kissed, and invited to sit on thick rugs. The women of the household were seated in a circle, facing a TV.

"The drama will be on soon," Freshta whispered. "The drama" turned out to be a TV soap opera from India, complete with rolling eyes, exclamations, sparkling saris, and glorious music, all dubbed in Dari.

I'd traveled halfway around the world—and there I was, sitting on a carpet watching a Bollywood *As the World Turns.*

toward the goal

KABUL, JULY 2007

"Patience is bitter, but it has a sweet fruit."
—AFGHAN PROVERB

VERY FRIDAY I was in Afghanistan, I made it to the Roots of Peace field for the girls' practice. One afternoon, I arrived early. Ariana and Robina were already there. I watched them as they laid their school backpacks against the wall, removed their head scarves, and folded them in their bags. They peeled off their nylon jackets and stood erect in their blue-and-black soccer uniforms, surveying the field like officers before a battle. It was almost synchronized.

Then they burst onto the field. I'd witnessed this many times, their running, reveling in their own sheer physical exertion. It was something I'd felt too before a game—a sense of calm coexisting with a rush of anticipation.

As more girls arrived and joined Ariana and Robina on the field, I heard someone call my name: "Awista *jan!*" I turned around. It was Miriam. Her brother Daud had brought her, knowing I'd be there. He was letting her come to practice— but only to watch. After he left, I turned to Miriam. "Miriam *jan,* it is just so good to see you!"

She looked full into my face. Her dark eyes brimmed with tears. There was great emotion in her. I knew what Daud had said. But in her face was something I loved, some- thing I wanted to respond to.

I pointed to the field. "Why don't you play?" She shook her head. "Come on!" I urged. She hesitated, pointing to her sandals. "We'll get you some cleats."

When I came back with the cleats, she stood up and ran out into the open ground. She raced to the ball and kicked a hard pass to Ariana, who dribbled it forward. There wasn't a goalie, though.

Fawad, the coach, came over. "I can protect the net," I told him. He nodded, "Go ahead." I crouched at the goal and clapped my hands. "Let's go!" I yelled. Except for a few scrimmages with the girls in America, I hadn't really played soccer with them. Now, here I was *in Afghanistan,* bouncing on the balls of my Nikes, yelling, "Goal, let's make a goal!" like one of the team.

I batted away a few shots, and was ready to stay at net all day. But the heat from the sun was intense. One by one, the girls drifted to the sidelines. I wiped sweat from my forehead and joined them.

It was surreal. My body was there, while my mind seemed to float over us, as if filming the scene from above. I thought of my parents. All the years they longed for the homeland.

And now, after weeks of being in Afghanistan, this was the moment that I'd felt it: at home.

A breeze stirred the grass. Quiet, I sat with my teammates.

The next morning, I woke early. I was excited. I was sad. I would be leaving Kabul in two days.

Today was the day of AYSE's girls' tournament.

It was scheduled to begin at 2 P.M., but I arrived hours earlier to make sure of every final detail. Fifteen teams would be competing, more than two hundred girls, among them members of the Women's National Team.

Armed guards were everywhere, lining the road to the military field and clustered at the entrance of International Security Assistance Force (ISAF) base. I made it through the gates and stepped onto the green field.

Teams began to arrive. Some girls still wore their school uniforms, with bags of equipment in tow. They rushed to their designated locker room to change.

Soon players emerged in long pants and loose T-shirts down to their elbows. A few wore their *hijabs* clipped under their chin so they wouldn't fall off during the game. Others had donned baseball caps.

Freshta and Laila had left for the United States, following Duaine, to visit him and Barbara. Only Ariana and Robina were left to compete. They were now on the same team— *Atma*. The Only One.

Robina and Ariana stood on the sidelines watching the other teams critically—their fumbling plays and slow, cautious passes.

"They are . . . not so good," Ariana said, wrinkling her nose. "They were good, but now people are watching."

Wind whipped up dust. The winning teams cheered as each short-sided game was completed. Winners of each bracket advanced into the final rounds, waiting for their next opponent along the sidelines or in the blue metal stands overlooking the field.

Ariana and Robina took the field in their blue-and-black striped uniforms, Robina sporting a dark bandana. It quickly became clear that their *Atma* team was a powerhouse. They pressured their opponents, stripping the ball easily and then powering toward the goal with long, quick strides. They passed to one another seamlessly, with few, if any, interceptions.

At one point in that match, the goalkeeper from the opposing team stopped the ball and kept it, running forward and taking her own shot. When she missed she jogged back.

I wanted to laugh. We'd been through *that* before!

The game continued. Robina, a more reckless player than Ariana, expended herself faster. She accelerated past other players, but her shots sometimes swerved wide. Ariana conserved her energy.

The team pressed onward. Ariana intercepted a pass. Then she nudged a straight, sure pass, threading it through the tangled bodies of the other team, right to her teammate. A few plays later, she lifted a long, smooth kick into the goal.

Atma won, 2–0.

"Who will believe it!" said an advisor from the German Football Project.

I knew the Afghan girls' sports program had a long way to go. But one thing was unmistakable. Eight players were now hundreds. Through organizations like the Afghanistan

Football Federation, girls stood proudly on their own country's field, more than 250 strong.

❧❀☙

I LEFT THE field. The coaches and I loaded the van with soccer equipment and a mound of balls. Zia made our way along the main avenue past Massoud Circle. We waited at the busy intersection near Wazir Akbar Khan, manned by traffic guards. There were few traffic lights.

A pile of soccer balls, all various colors, was easily seen through the truck's windows. As our van neared the front of the traffic line, I saw familiar faces—a young boy begging, his sister right behind him. I'd seen them the day before.

They both approached our van, his hand held out. Then his sister saw the soccer balls and her eyes lit up.

"*Lutfan, man metanam yak top'a bigiram kaka jan?*" she asked my driver through the open window.

Zia turned around in his seat. "She's asking for a ball. Can we give her one?"

"Of course!" I said and passed one up to him, along with some money.

"Zia *jan*, please offer them a few afghanis too," I said.

But the girl and boy refused the money, waving it off. The girl held the ball instead, smiling.

As we continued driving, I turned around in my seat and looked through the back window. The girl with the ball and her brother and their friends were in a huddle. They began to play.

The girl kicked the ball. It arced upward.

epilogue

N AFGHANISTAN NO one I spoke with embraced the Taliban or had enjoyed life under their regime. But I did meet brothers who thought their sisters should stay at home and not go to school, and high-ranking sports officials who questioned whether girls' soccer could be reconciled with religion.

In the center were girls who considered themselves Muslim. They prayed daily, respected scriptures, dressed modestly. However, they also wanted to be educated, pursue careers, marry men they loved at a time they chose, and to play soccer—or any sport—without asking permission. They would eagerly seize every opportunity given to them.

For society at large the question had become: What opportunities should be offered? And at what pace?

That depended on whom you asked.

IN 2005, WHILE I was working at the Embassy of Afghanistan in Washington, D.C., all the news was about a young female basketball player determined to win a seat in that year's parliamentary elections—it seemed unreal, even more so when she won.

Sabrina Saqib, at twenty-seven, was one of the youngest members of the Afghanistan Parliament.

I met with her on my trip to Afghanistan in 2007. On the day of our interview, a burly security man greeted me. Like every Parliamentarian, Sabrina had an armed guard assigned to her. He led the way up five flights of stairs, past the broken elevators, with their call buttons smashed.

As Sabrina welcomed me into her apartment, the guard took up his post outside her door.

Sabrina was born in Kabul in the late 1970s. Her parents immigrated to Iran when she was a child. She went on to graduate from Tehran University, where she played basketball in female-only gymnasiums.

Iran had created one model for female sports participation in an Islamic country. Their stable athletic infrastructure included women's coaches, trainers, and referees—as well as dedicated gymnasiums where girls and women could compete in a female-only environment. These gender-segregated arenas provided a way for women to play sports, while also respecting the culture.

In 2001, Sabrina returned to Kabul and looked for basketball programs for women. There weren't any.

"So I did the only sensible thing," she told me. "I joined a men's basketball team."

For practice games, Sabrina and the male players tried to avoid any physical contact—hard in a sport where contact is the norm. It meant the men couldn't really guard her. Even though there were no public games, and Sabrina dressed in loose shirts and long pants, people talked. After a while, one of her teammates told her: "Please, you can't come anymore. Your presence is causing too many problems for us."

"I wasn't surprised," Sabrina said.

As luck would have it, soon after, Sabrina was invited to help start a women's basketball program through the ANABF (Afghanistan National Amateur Basketball Federation). Although the program expanded to include hundreds of girls across Kabul, many players dropped out, stopped by marriage, husbands, or family pressure.

So Sabrina spoke directly to the families themselves.

"We have to have strong women," she'd tell them. "If women want to be good mothers, fit mothers, sports can help. For healthy children, it's not just enough to go to the doctor—if the mother has exercised, it can help her to have strong children." She was appealing to what many families felt was the main responsibility of women.

Sometimes there was nothing to be done.

"We have to let the girls come and go, come and go. One day they will stay forever."

Did the struggle for a women's sports program prepare her for her run for political office? Definitely.

In 2004, Afghanistan's first parliamentary elections in thirty-five years were being organized. Sabrina's mother encouraged her to run.

She was twenty-six years old.

Colored posters with a photo of Sabrina were plastered throughout Kabul. In them, she wore a yellow *hijab* and smiled directly into the camera. Young people in particular were so enamored with the posters that many were stolen and pasted up in their homes.

Some, though, found her poster too forward. It was very different than the typical black-and-white photo of a grim-faced candidate, surrounded with dense text.

On September 18, 2005, millions of Afghans made it to the polls to cast their vote. According to the 2004 Constitution, 25 percent of the parliament—sixty-eight seats—was reserved for women. When the results were in, seventy-four women had won their districts, accounting for 28 percent of the seats in parliament. Sabrina was one of them.

Sabrina Saqib is determined to create opportunities for women through sports in Afghanistan. "Sports are a sign of peace in Afghanistan," she said. "Step by step, we will have both."

⟨❧⟩

SHUKRIA HAKMAT, THIRTY-NINE, is the deputy for Afghan women's participation in the Olympics. I interviewed her, aptly enough, at Ghazi Stadium. She was just completing her first year in the women's office, managing eighteen women's sport's programs.

Shukria remembered the thriving sports program she'd grown up with—competitive teams, Western sports clothing, intensive coaching, and stands packed for the games, with men and women cheering. She herself played basketball during this time, in the early seventies.

With war, she and her husband left for Pakistan, and returned to Kabul in 2002. The state of women's sports then came as a shock.

"The day I came, there was nothing. At the first practices in Ghazi Stadium, the girls were barefoot. They didn't have the sneakers or the right kind of clothing. We had to start everything from the ground up."

At the time, she said, people were "very *bay-tarbya,* dark-minded."

Even so, Shukria was encouraged. Slowly, "people are more open and accepting toward women playing sports."

Bit by bit, she and her office were piecing together sports opportunities for women within the Olympic Committee. It was still a struggle, however. Like Sabrina Saqib, Shukria Hakmat frequently visited families, personally encouraging them to let their daughters play. It was slow going, with a notable success here and there.

"Deena's a volleyball player. A really good one. At first, her husband wouldn't let her play," Shukria told me.

Shukria visited Deena's husband and family, appealing to their nationalism. "If you let Deena play, you will be making a contribution to our country," she told them.

They agreed.

Then Deena's volleyball team made it to the championship game of the Volleyball Federation's tournament. The game would be televised. This was another obstacle, but Shukria overcame it.

Shukria understood that change would be wrought slowly.

"I respect all views," she said softly. "But we can find a middle way."

The middle way, according to Shukria, was female-only gymnasiums. Until then, Shukria would continue visiting homes one by one, convincing parents, husbands, and in-laws to let women play.

"I have a dream, more important than where athletes play or the uniforms they wear," she said. "One day we will get Olympic medals. Until then I will never leave my country. I will never stop."

❦

IF SABRINA SAQIB and Shukria Hakmat saw women's sports as a sign of peace and progress in Afghanistan, Safiullah Subat represented both its hope and obstacle. When I interviewed him, he had been the chief of physical education for the Afghanistan Ministry of Education for six years.

An accomplished soccer player, Safiullah's government job came not long after the fall of the Taliban. Now in his sixties, he'd played soccer for more than forty years.

Regarding sports in Afghanistan, his opinion was that slow progress was best. "We should have a limited number of sports federations, and they should be ones that we can put more focus and attention on," he said.

Which sports? Four: soccer, boxing, wrestling, and track and field.

In response to a query about volleyball, a popular sport for girls, he replied, "I believe volleyball is a very ordinary game, and even if you go to the most remote area in the country, you will find people playing volleyball there." The implication was that since it was played everywhere, a federation for it wasn't necessary.

"For some sports, women are physically not ready or it's not appropriate for them," he said. "For example, boxing, weight lifting, soccer. Physically, they are not good for women. I believe a woman's body, by nature, is weaker as compared to a man's. Allah created women to be very delicate."

Safiullah leaned forward. "If I give you this ball, would you be able to break the glass?" he asked. "Even though I'm twice your age, if I throw this ball on the wall, that wall would shake," he continued. "But you wouldn't be able to break the window glass. It doesn't mean that women are less capable than men."

This question of strength has been debated throughout the world. In many countries, there isn't a sport women haven't tried, or, for that matter, excelled in.

However, Safiullah's thinking was common, especially among older Afghan men, whether in America or Afghanistan.

"I am not against women in sports," he added firmly. "But, for example, men in our society do not want their women to go bareheaded to play soccer. They want them covered. You know that for soccer players it's very important to wear shorts. If you wear long pants, you won't be able to shoot as well."

Safiullah knew about the work of the Afghan Youth Sports Exchange and my role in it, so he clarified his position. "I don't mean that women should not play soccer. Since I am a soccer player myself, I would never stop the advancement of soccer in any way for any type of purpose."

His only concern was to find the right conditions for them to play.

"I want them to be in their own separate gymnasium . . . among themselves. I want them to play soccer, but in their own area, with women trainers."

Safiullah stressed that there had to be a process. "No one

will be happy if we go from zero to sixty overnight," he said. It was just a few years ago, under the Taliban, that he had had a long beard, women weren't allowed in school, and executions took place on the same field where women played soccer today.

"How would it be possible, after what we went through, for women to already be out in the stadium, wearing shorts and competing while men watch along the sideline? If I take it too fast, and I do everything too quickly, then reactions will come and [girls' sports] will stop completely. The community will stand against it and they will ban the whole thing for good."

As if he'd heard a protest, he pressed on: "I know my people and the situation in my country—that is why I am telling you that it's important to go slowly, respect the culture and the situation in the country right now." During the thirty years the United States was implementing Title IX, Afghanistan was overtaken by a different history. The year the U.S. women won the World Cup, the Taliban took Kabul. After years of war and destruction, Safiullah seemed to be saying that time would be needed to rebuild, to heal.

⚜

IT SEEMED THAT the "slow pace" referred to by Safiullah Subat, and the resistance to progress in this area outlined by Sabrina Saqib and Shukria Hakmat, found voice and reality in the experience of Abdul Saboor Walizada. Walizada, the Women's National Team head coach, and I had worked together on the girls' soccer clinic and tournament in Kabul.

Twenty-five girls represented Afghanistan on the National

Team. Although all the players hailed from Kabul, Walizada—what he prefers to be called—had plans to expand beyond the capital and establish a truly national team.

His work has been marked by extraordinary success, and controversy. In some ways he has been the pivotal person in women's soccer.

"People laugh at me for training women and mock me for what I am doing," Walizada said. "I can't say that I am completely comfortable with my position for that reason. I do get public harassment."

Even younger generations of Afghan men were not ready, or willing, to accept a man coaching a women's sports team, he believed.

But that was the least of it.

Six months after he started coaching the women's team, Walizada had been pulled from his car and beaten up by two armed men. He was not surprised by the attack, and referred to it in an offhand manner. Violence in the country was ubiquitous, and Walizada was only glad he hadn't been seriously hurt.

"I never found out who they were or their reasons," he said. "Maybe I was training their sister or somebody from their family without their permission, I don't know. After that, I wanted to drop this work, but we'd had some progress with the program, and my colleagues wanted me to continue."

At one point, a group of boys and men scaled the wall to *Bagh-e-Zanana*, the Women's Garden, as the team was practicing, and hurled stones at the girls. Military personnel manning one of their practice fields taunted Walizada, and once, at a tournament, outraged university students tried to storm the field.

"Bright, open-minded, educated people," Walizada said with a weary smile. "I am very tired. I'm tired of the continuous struggle . . . sometimes it is beyond my tolerance. But still, I love soccer."

꧁꧂

SINCE I RETURNED to the United States, the Afghan girls' team has competed in the Women's National Soccer League tournament in Pakistan—making it all the way to the championship game, which took place in late August 2007. They finished second in a field of four teams, just behind Pakistan's national team.

They had never played a full field 11 versus 11 game before, and never played outside Afghanistan before this tournament.

Robina, the team's co-captain, was the top scorer in the tournament.

As this book goes to press, Afghanistan has yet to field a women's Olympic team in soccer, but the Afghanistan Football Federation has been working to get the team FIFA (Fédération Internationale de Football Association) ranked.

꧁꧂

NOT A DAY goes by that I don't think of Robina, Ariana, Freshta, Laila, Samira, Miriam, Deena, and Nadia. Their visit to the States and my journey to my homeland are merged together in my mind into a clear picture of them running after the ball, their laughter echoing over the walls, into the bright, clear air.

Sometimes all it takes is one ball and many dreams.

Acknowledgments

IT WAS GRETCHEN YOUNG of Hyperion who first reached out to me and brought this book to fruition. Thank you for believing in this story of struggle, hope, and courage. To my agent, Heather Mitchell, who was the book's tireless champion when not a word yet was written and whose passion kept the book alive, never allowing me to lose hope—thank you.

As always, to my family, who are the source of inspiration in my own life—my parents, Mohammad Hassan Ayub and Bibi Aissa Ayub (Gulalai), and siblings, Hiwad John Ayub and Zohra Ayub—thank you. I wouldn't be where I am today without the dedication and support you have given me over the years.

In my own work toward supporting women's soccer in Afghanistan, there have been countless individuals and organizations who have helped and supported me every step of the way in a true team effort. I am grateful to all of you, as your own belief in me has served to fuel the fire and vision I had.

Duaine and Barbara Goodno, who took the risk in believing in me in 2004 when all I had was an idea on paper—as I've come to know you more over the years, I have witnessed your generous spirit shine through.

To the coaches who traveled to Kabul and organized the clinics on the ground—it is because of you that the programs in Afghanistan were possible—Sabina Rogers, Azita Munsif, Sohaila Qudus Alamyar, Khalid Alamyar, Arian Nawabi, Tareq Azim, Fatima Popal, Nancy Waite, Esmael Husseini, Mamo Rafiq, and Tariq Rafiq. You have given much and, I hope, gained much in return.

A deep sense of gratitude goes out to the various sponsors and supporters of AYSE over the years: ESPN—Kerri Johnson, Johnson McKelvy, and Scott Duncan; TriWest—David McIntyre and Jennifer Meyer; the Afghan Communicator—Rameen Moshref Javid and his staff; the Afghanistan National Olympic Committee; the Afghanistan Football Federation; the Afghanistan National Amateur Basketball Federation; the Afghanistan Ministry of Education; American Airlines; the Ethel Walker School—Kim Blanchard and her family; Simsbury Soccer Club—Jerry Garlick; the International Children's Games in Cleveland, Ohio—Carol Payto; the Afghan Sports Federation; the Embassy of Afghanistan and staff in Washington, D.C.; the U.S. Embassy in Kabul, Afghanistan—Elijah Waterman; Velocity Athletics; PeacePlayers International; the U.S. Soccer Foundation and their Passback Program; Kwik Goal; Pugg; Eurosport; Soccer Plus Camps—Tony DiCicco; Millennium Enterprises; and the Julie Foudy Sports Leadership Academy.

On a personal level, there are many others who have been true friends along the way and were always there to lend support to me, the program, and the book: Mariam Atash Nawabi and Alina Atash and their families. The entire Zaka family in Virginia, Jawed Sanie, Jamil Faryadi, Mariam Wardak and Mariam Ehsan, Dr. Riaz Rayek, Dr. Homaira Behsudi, Asiyah Sarwari Sharifi, Alix

Méav Ellinwood-Jerome, and David Pérez, whose comments and fresh ideas further helped strengthen the book.

Each one of my trips to Kabul was a memorable one, and this was due in large part to the help of two friends. Homira Nassery, who helped welcome me "home," providing both personal support and guidance in planning my trips. And Zia Haydari, who is, in my opinion, the best driver in Kabul!

Finally, to the many Afghan and American families who hosted the team while we were in Washington, D.C., and in Connecticut. Your hospitality was truly appreciated.

Most important, to the girls, for sharing their stories.

Reading Group Guide

1. In the beginning of the book, Awista writes that the hyphen in Afghan-American "includes and divides." What does she mean by this? How does her own journey bridge the divide between her Afghani and American lives?

2. Samira's extended family and her neighbors openly object to her going to America to play soccer. Why do you think her parents encourage her, despite the objections of those around them?

3. When Samira returns to Afghanistan after visiting America, she has a very hard time readjusting to her old life. Why is it so hard for her? What about America, and her friends, draws Samira away from her family and her country?

4. When Robina's friend Tamana is taken out of school by her family, she writes to Robina, "You're very lucky." Do you consider Robina lucky? Does she think she is lucky? After

reading this book, do you consider yourself more or less fortunate?

5. All the girls have a difficult time problem-solving peacefully and working as a team. Why is that? Why is it difficult for them to trust one another? Once they become a team, the bond is very important to them. What does the team offer each of them? What does being a team mean to them?

6. How is Ariana different from the other girls on the team? Is she more independent? Stronger? Why is Ariana switching to another team such a betrayal to the rest of the girls?

7. What does it mean for the girls' soccer team to play in Ghazi Stadium? How is it significant to them? How is it significant to the entire nation of Afghanistan?

8. Why do you think Awista is so motivated to bring sports to the girls of Afghanistan? Do you think it is a worthwhile goal? Why or why not? What can be gained by giving children the opportunity to play sports?

9. What did you learn about Afghanistan from reading this book? Did any of the country's history surprise you?

A Conversation with Awista Ayub

Q: *What is the Afghan Youth Sports Exchange (AYSE) and why did you decide to bring young Afghan women to the States to play soccer?*

A: The Afghan Youth Sports Exchange (AYSE) is an organization I founded in late 2003 dedicated to equipping Afghanistan's youth with the leadership skills required to promote athletics in their communities. Bringing a group of female soccer players to the States for training, I thought, would provide them an opportunity to experience another culture and gain leadership skills while also learning the fundamentals of the sport.

I chose soccer not because of my love for the sport per se, but because of my impression of the global nature of the sport itself. Also, soccer is easy, since all you really need to play is a ball. The goal was that the girls, upon their return to Afghanistan, would help teach soccer to other young children in Afghanistan. What I would come to understand later, though, was that by choosing soccer, a male-dominated sport in Afghanistan, the girls would be pushing the boundaries of the sports culture and would be thrust into a position that would challenge the gender barriers of the culture both on and off the field.

Q: *How did you find a group of young Afghan girls interested in playing soccer? Was it difficult to convince their families to allow them to travel to America?*

A: A colleague on the ground in Kabul found the first group of girls that traveled to the States in 2004. Since girls weren't playing soccer at the time that we were recruiting, the decision in choosing each girl was based on their own level of maturity in being able to handle a trip to the States. We also based it on their leadership potential, as we hoped the girls would help teach peers the sport upon their return to Afghanistan.

Getting permission from the parents was not actually too difficult. I strongly believe that parents all over the world want to provide what is best for their children, regardless if it's their daughters or sons and regardless of what country they live in. By the time of the program, Afghanistan had faced over twenty-five years of war and violence, dating back to 1978. The girls were born into this world of brutality. When a chance came for them to participate in the exchange trip to the States, their parents were more than happy to allow their daughters to see the world beyond their troubled region.

Q: *Why do you think the Afghan girls were argumentative when they first arrived in the States?*

A: I think that for those of us who grew up outside of a conflict zone, it is difficult to understand the overwhelming impact that growing up in a culture of war can have. War brought violence and conflict to their lives on a daily basis. Certainly, living under these circumstances impacted how they dealt with issues in their own lives. As they were used to seeing issues resolved through arguments, butting heads was their initial reaction in dealing with conflict—both on and off the field. And while they also didn't participate in organized sports until their trip to the States, I think the soccer field became a place where they could change their behavior and learn how best to deal with conflict. So while I was initially surprised by the arguments, I came to better understand where it stemmed from.

Q: *In 1996, the U.S. women's soccer team competed for the World Cup. That same year the Taliban took over Kabul. How have women's rights changed in Afghanistan since then?*

A: Rights for women in Afghanistan have gone through a roller coaster of ups and downs throughout the country's rich history. Afghan women living in the larger cities like Kabul and Kandahar up until 1978 had experienced a great deal of freedom—working outside of the home, choosing what they wanted for their lives. My mother frequently shared with me such stories of liberated women in our homeland. For me, the initial image of a "repressed Afghan woman" is not the first thing that comes to mind, which it sadly does for many who've only recently come to learn about Afghanistan.

There were low points for both women and men during the period from 1996 to 2001, which has sadly become the only history of Afghans that most people associate with the country. Opportunities for women and men during the past thirty years of war were limited, and more so for women who weren't allowed to work or go to school from 1996 to 2001, while the Taliban had control of the country. Today, opportunities for young Afghans, both girls and boys, have increased, with millions of students returning to school throughout the country. While women are entering the workforce in larger numbers, they are still navigating the country's new cultural identity, and we must keep in mind that change takes time.

Q: *Has the empowerment of women in Afghanistan influenced women in Iran and other parts of the Middle East?*

A: I would say that it is actually the other way around. Up to now, women in other Muslim countries have probably had more opportunities compared to Afghan women, given the nature of the war and violence that overtook the country since 1978. Although women in some Muslim countries may be physically covered, this is not enough to judge the level of rights and opportunities they might have, as every country is different in their level of women's rights. Change, in regard to women's rights, is a tricky subject . . . I think those of us who grew up in the States might be quick to judge or want to influence the lives of women locally in other countries. We must be aware, though, that it is not our choice or our place to decide what is best for them. Change must take place locally and be driven by Afghan women in order for it to ever take hold in the long term. With that, though, as women gain more strength, courage, and education, they will become more vocal and direct about what they want in life.

More specifically, in looking at the sports culture of women in other Muslim countries, girls are participating in sports at various levels, and are doing so in spaces reserved for women only. This is the case in Iran and Morocco. In this regard, while Afghanistan is still struggling to find its own sports identity, they can learn how to respect the culture and still provide a space for women by learning from other Muslim countries.

Q: *Do you have plans to bring this sports exchange to more girls in Afghanistan?*

A: While the first program I organized in 2004 was an exchange of players to the States, I have since traveled to Kabul with a delegation of Afghan-American coaches in 2006 and 2007, working with the local sports federations on the ground toward implementing girls' sports clinics. In working locally in Afghanistan, I found that the program can have a large impact on young girls on the ground.

While I think a sports exchange program does have its benefits, it must be coupled with a longer term sustainable vision as well. Programs that incorporate an exchange must follow it up with a long-term project that those participants can implement locally, so that there is an impact on others at the local level and not only on those few who participated in the exchange.

Q: *What can readers do to help support women's rights and access to sports around the world?*

A: In regard to AYSE, the last in-country program we were able to do took place during the summer of 2007. As security has increasingly become an issue, I couldn't guarantee the safety of those coaches that traveled with the program to Kabul. While my work, up to now, has focused solely on Afghanistan, I've also come to understand that more funding and support also needs to be provided for more Muslim women's sports programs in other countries. With this in mind, I've partnered with the Dutch NGO Women Win in starting the However Tall the Mountain Fund, in which funds will be used to support programs for Muslim women in sports. More information is available at www.awistaayub .com.

Q: *What was the most surprising thing you learned from this experience (from talking to the girls, doing research, visiting Afghanistan, etc.)?*

A: The most surprising thing that I learned from this experience was the role of sports in Afghanistan, particularly soccer. As I grew up in the States, I came to view soccer as a gender neutral sport with equal, if not more, participation from women, and so I thought soccer was a universal sport that women were equally participating in throughout the world. It wasn't until after the girls returned home, after the summer in 2004, and upon my own subsequent trips to Afghanistan, that I came to understand how polarizing an issue it is to have had women playing soccer. Not only are female soccer players in Afghanistan pushing against years of cultural barriers that girls face on a daily basis, but they are also pushing the cultural norm for the sport itself in Afghanistan and redefining the role of women within that sports arena.

Q: *Ghazi Stadium in Kabul is an iconic place—once the site of national sports competitions, the space was nearly destroyed during years of war in Afghanistan. What must it have meant for the girls to play there?*

A: From talking with the female soccer players in Afghanistan, I would say that the opportunity to play in their national stadium, Ghazi, is very much an honor that they cherish. The Ghazi Stadium, since it was built in 1923, was always a venue filled with joy and national pride. Now, though, it has sadly become synonymous with the executions that took place there. Today those images should be replaced with what is taking place there now—young women and men playing sports on the national stage for their country. Sports, I feel, has amazing potential to help restore the cultural identity of a country, particularly a post-conflict country.

Awista Ayub was born in Afghanistan and immigrated to the United States in 1981. She founded the Afghan Youth Sports Exchange and served as the Education and Health Officer at the Embassy of Afghanistan in Washington, D.C. Awista received her Bachelor of Science degree in Chemistry from the University of Rochester and her Master of Public Administration from the University of Delaware. Awista was a Women Win fellow, and is now an ambassador for the organization.